The Global Oil Market
Risks and Uncertainties

The Global Oil Market
Risks and Uncertainties

Anthony H. Cordesman and Khalid R. Al-Rodhan

THE CSIS PRESS

Center for Strategic
and International Studies
Washington, D.C.

Significant Issues Series, Volume 28, Number 1

10 09 08 07 06   5 4 3 2 1

ISSN: 0736-7136
ISBN-13: 978-0-89206-479-3
ISBN-10: 0-89206-479-X

Library of Congress Cataloging-in-Publication Data
Cordesman, Anthony H.
    The global oil market : risks and uncertainties / Anthony H.
Cordesman and Khalid R. Al-Rodhan.
        p. cm. — (Significant issues series ; v. 28, no. 1)
    Includes bibliographical references.
    ISBN-13: 978-0-89206-479-3 (pbk. : alk. paper)
    ISBN-10: 0-89206-479-X (pbk. : alk. paper)
    1. Petroleum industry and trade—Economic aspects. 2. Petroleum
industry and trade—Political aspects. 3. Petroleum products—Prices.
4. Energy policy.   I. Al-Rodhan, Khalid R. II. Title. III. Series.
HD9560.5.C588 2006
338.2'7282—dc22
                                        2006003324

CONTENTS

TABLES AND FIGURES

Tables

Figures

ACKNOWLEDGMENTS

The authors would like to thank many government officials, energy experts, and strategic analysts for their comments on a draft of this book. Special thanks go to two colleagues at CSIS, Bates Gill and Peter DeShazo, for their invaluable comments and suggestions. The authors relied on the assistance and research of Emily Fall.

AUTHORS' NOTES

This book relies on many sources, including reports by the U.S. Energy Information Administration (EIA), the International Energy Agency (IEA), the Organization of the Petroleum Exporting Countries (OPEC), and the U.S. Geological Survey (USGS); reports from energy companies such as Aramco and BP; news articles; and reports by energy analysts. Data and analysis for oil supply and demand were adapted from reports such as the EIA's *International Energy Outlook 2005* and the IEA's *World Energy Outlook 2005*. Reserve data were adapted from two main sources: BP's *Statistical Review of World Energy 2005* and the USGS *U.S. Geological Survey 2000*.

The definitions of three key terms can be summarized as follows:

- *Known reserves:* discovered crude oil accumulations that are considered economically viable to produce

- *Proven reserves:* quantities of crude oil that geological data and engineering information indicate with reasonable certainty can be recovered in the future

- *Undiscovered reserves:* quantities of crude oil that geological data and engineering information indicate exist outside known oil fields.

The acronym *mmbpd* for million barrels per day is used throughout the text.

CHAPTER ONE

———

OVERVIEW

The future of energy is of enormous importance, and the global flow of oil is a critical component of both the world's energy supply and global economic growth and stability. Yet, it is clear that the global energy market is intricate and the analysis of it is uncertain. The ability of policy planners and strategists in oil-consuming nations to control risk is limited at best. Most of the world's known oil reserves exist in regions and countries that are not stable. Consumers cannot control where reserves exist, and the geostrategic risks are not likely to change in the near future.

The dynamics of the current oil market involve four major interdependent areas of uncertainty: geostrategic risks, macroeconomic fluctuations, the nature of resource risks, and the uncertainty of current and future oil-production capacity.

At this point, about all that is certain about the forces shaping the world's energy supply is that the global energy market is unpredictable and that recent oil prices have been high and volatile. In four years, the price per barrel of oil has increased by roughly 108 percent. Rigorous, transparent, and credible analysis, however, can improve our understanding of the forces at play and provide policymakers and analysts with the tools necessary to forge sound energy policy based on real-world realities and risks.

KEY GEOPOLITICAL UNCERTAINTIES

The six major petroleum-producing regions (the Middle East, Africa, Asia and the Pacific, Europe and Eurasia, North America, and Latin

America) face major production and resource uncertainties. It is clear that the geostrategic risks facing these regions have tangible implications for both their energy sectors and the global petroleum market. The geopolitical and military implications are hard to quantify. But it is clear that the risk premium of these uncertainties will be affected by the following key geostrategic challenges, all of which could have direct and indirect effects on the global energy market:

- *The stability of oil- and gas-exporting nations*: The stability of oil- and gas-producing nations is of paramount importance for the world oil and gas market. The strikes in Venezuela, the war in Iraq, and the ongoing disruptions of Angolan and Nigerian oil are examples of what could happen if there was instability in other countries such as Saudi Arabia and Iran.

- *Terrorism in the Gulf and the security of oil facilities*: Although the threat from Iran's conventional military may be real, the more dangerous threat may be from extremists groups' asymmetric attacks on oil facilities. The Persian Gulf contains over 65 percent of the world's "proven" reserves. There is no attack-proof security system. It could take only one asymmetric or conventional attack on Saudi Arabia's Ghawar oil field or on tankers in the Strait of Hormuz to throw the market into a spiral, at least for the near future.

- *Proliferation of weapons of mass destruction*: The success in stopping the A. Q. Khan black-market network does not mean the end of a nuclear black market. There remains a real threat to the entire world, especially in the Gulf, of a nuclear weapon falling into "the wrong hands," such as Al Qaeda.

- *Embargoes and sanctions*: Another oil embargo by the Organization of the Petroleum Exporting Countries (OPEC) is unlikely. But if oil or gas exports were ever used as weapons to combat U.S. or Western foreign policy—or if sanctions were imposed on Iran, for example—it might have a major effect on the global economy.

- *Ethnic conflicts and sectarian strife:* Disagreements over the control of oil revenues by ethnic tribal, religious, and other factions can destabilize countries and disrupt the flow of oil and gas.

Additional geostrategic challenges include security problems and accidents, as well as natural disasters that occur in production, export, or refining areas. These will be discussed in detail in chapter 2. All such challenges can have unpredictable effects on price and supply that have an impact on the entire global economy.

MACROECONOMIC FLUCTUATIONS

Like all economic forecasts, predicting supply, demand, and prices of crude oil involves significant uncertainty. Predicting the oil market is notoriously difficult, and constant updates and additions to the models are needed. The most recent forecasts by the U.S. Energy Information Administration (EIA), the International Energy Agency (IEA), and OPEC have not been adjusted to fully consider the impact of long-term oil prices in the $50 and above range—even in their high-oil-price case. Only the EIA's global forecasts have as yet partially addressed high-price cases for petroleum, and these forecasts do not examine the influence that high oil prices would have on the demand, supply, and the long-term elasticity of global energy balances.

Several key factors influence the oil market, and each involves major uncertainties and unknowns:

- *The long-term elasticity of oil and gas supply:* Major debates exist over the size of proven, possible, and potential resources' rates of discovery, development and production costs, oil fields' life spans, and the impact of advanced technology.

- *The overall health of the global economy:* The influence of oil prices on the global economy is all too clear in many ways. Sustained high oil prices have a marked negative effect on economic growth in oil-consuming states and tend to slow global economic growth. In addition, low economic growth in industrialized nations and consuming nations causes a decrease in demand for oil and hence lower oil prices.

- *The rise of new economic powers:* In recent years, the oil market has experienced an unexpected increase in demand from countries in Asia such as China and India. Emerging Asian and Middle Eastern economies also are driving the high demand for oil. According to the International Monetary Fund (IMF), this surge from emerging economies could account for 40 percent of the increase in oil demand in 2004.

- *Lack of investment:* These pressures and uncertainties add to the economic risk premium, causing oil prices to rise further. Moreover, though higher oil prices may provide incentives for private and public investment in the oil industry, the lack of geopolitical stability and an inability to predict how long high oil prices will continue prevent many from investing in these areas. Meeting the kind of massive surges in the demand for oil projected in recent studies will require massive investments to build new infrastructure and finance new technologies.

Other key factors include

- problems in import-dependent developing countries;
- the sustainable and spare capacity of oil- and gas-producing countries;
- the cost of sustaining and expanding oil and gas production and exports, and of the necessary investments;
- country capability and practice in sustaining and expanding oil and gas production and exports;
- substitution and the long-term elasticity of demand; and
- the refining capacity and inventory buildup of importing nations.

Each of these factors is treated in detail in chapter 3.

THE NATURE OF RESOURCE RISKS

Given the strategic risks faced by oil-producing nations, claims about production goals and capacity and oil reserves have long been a political tool. Limited hard data are available to validate many national claims and plans. Yet credibility in this area is of enormous importance because, as we will see, key modelers depend on each country's reports for their demand-driven models to forecast global supply and demand. In many cases, data are lacking, there is little validation or transparency, and current models and estimates simply assume levels of petroleum capacity that may never exist.

The global energy market faces key uncertainties in determining the exact nature of reserves, including the following:

- *The true nature of reserves:* There are ongoing debates on the reliability of estimates of different types of reserves. The *U.S. Geological Survey 2000* continues to be the benchmark estimate. However, as with any estimates, forecasting is uncertain. Furthermore, analysts disagree about the definition of "known" versus "undiscovered" versus "proven" resources.

- *The impact of technological gain:* Technological uncertainties affect every aspect of oil exploration, production, and exporting. Some experts argue that aging oil fields have higher water cuts and that "vertical" wells cannot be used. Other energy estimates do not take into account new technological developments, which may change the estimates of "possible" and "probable" reserves. Similar technological issues affect estimates of "refining creep" and gas exploration, production, and export technology.

- *The ability to substitute for current supergiant and giant fields:* Some experts have argued that new field discoveries do not support reserve estimates, and that major producers such as Saudi Arabia, Iraq, Kuwait, and the United Arab Emirates rely on aging supergiant fields that were discovered in the 1950s and 1960s and are in decline, with none of their kind having been found in recent years.

- *Rate of decline in fields:* The percentage of the oil reserves in the fields that have been pumped out is a contentious and uncertain estimate. Analysts and investors have to rely on independent estimates and announcements by exporting nations and oil and gas companies.

- *Rate and size of new developments and discoveries:* Outside analysts have to rely on the discovering country's announcement and statement for estimates of any new discoveries. Moreover, it remains uncertain whether certain countries are "overexplored" or "underexplored."

- *Inaccuracy of three-dimensional seismic modeling:* Some experts have argued that new technologies using computer models are not enough. They provide a good estimate of possible reserves, but they do not replace old-fashioned drilling and physically measuring actual reserves.

- *National efficiency and decisionmaking capabilities:* Countries and national companies differ in their decisionmaking and efficiency in exploring for new reserves. In addition, countries have adopted radically different reservoir management systems that directly affect the nature of reserves in those reservoirs. How well these systems work depends on the countries' knowledge of technological developments and on national companies' willingness to adopt those changes

- *Politicization of reserves:* Petroleum- and gas-producing nations tend to politicize their reserves to project strategic importance. This adds to the lack of transparency and credibility, which is hard to overcome.

In many cases, it is not clear that the EIA, IEA, OPEC, or the U.S. Geological Survey (USGS) have applied sufficient rigor to a country-by-country examination of such estimates. (The USGS does use a different methodology because it looks at the basins on a geological potential basis, but the data available are uncertain and dated.)

THE LACK OF ROBUST MODELING

Modeling is urgently needed to examine supply-driven models, not just demand-driven models. Many laypeople do not understand the wide range of problems in the foundations on which forecasting methodology are based. It is all too clear, however, that the modeling the EIA, IEA, and OPEC have used in forecasting global petroleum supply and demand has been driven by estimating global oil demand at comparatively low prices.

Reports by the EIA, IEA, and OPEC could provide a better benchmark for the global energy market if they addressed certain areas of deficiency. Chapter 2 will examine the key gaps and areas of uncertainty in the *International Energy Outlook 2005*. These include the following:

- lack of parametric analysis;
- insufficient attention to the effects of economic growth rates;
- no attention to country-by-country plans in forecasting oil production capacity;
- insufficient analysis of indirect imports;
- insufficient analysis of the impact of technological improvements on national oil and gas production and export capacity;
- little transparency in showing the relation of oil prices to demand for alternatives and conservation;
- little effort to explain, justify, and parametrically model the different elasticity patterns in supply and demand for gas, coal, nuclear power, renewables, electricity, and conservation that have to emerge over time if oil prices remain so much higher than in the past, or the inevitable major uncertainties that will result from such changes; and
- use of unrealistic smooth curves and largely "static" assumptions for the models and forecasts.

Because of these gaps, the current forecasts of EIA, IEA, and OPEC do little more than illustrate what might happen if virtually everything goes right from the importer's view, export capacities automatically respond to need, and political and military risk have no impact.

OIL PRODUCTION UNCERTAINTIES

If the growing high demand for oil is sustained, almost all sources indicate that it will put a growing strain on both global oil supply and export capacity. BP's *Statistical Review of World Energy 2005* reported that in 2004, the average total world production was 80.26 million barrels per day (mmbpd)—higher than the 2003 average by 3.206 mmbpd. In 2004, OPEC produced 32.927 mmbpd, an increase of 7.7 percent above its 2003 production levels; Russia increased its production by 0.741 mmbpd (+8.9 percent); and China increased its by 0.089 mmbpd (+2.9 percent).[1]

Non-OPEC supply so far has been slow to respond to the high oil prices. In fact, it increased by only 0.046 mmbpd in 2004 (31.8 percent of which came from the Former Soviet Union). According to the U.S. Department of Energy, the expected increase in non-OPEC oil production for 2005 is 0.92 mmbpd.[2] In 2005 and 2006, more than half of this non-OPEC increase is estimated to come from the FSU and the Atlantic Basin, including Latin America and West Africa.[3]

The EIA forecasts total world production capacity in 2025 for the low-price, reference, and high-price cases as follows: 135.2 mmbpd for the low-price case, 122.2 mmbpd for the reference case, and 115.5 mmbpd for the high-price case. In both the 2004 and 2005 cases, the projected increase in total world production capacity is still significant. By 2010, it could increase from 14.6 mmbpd to as high as 21.6 mmbpd. The "high-price" case, however, is far easier to achieve in the real world than the "reference" or "low-price" cases.

As is clear from these numbers, as the price of oil decreases, production capacity increases. One notable exception is that non-OPEC countries' production capacities have the opposite reaction to a change in the price of oil. OPEC countries largely drive this relationship between price and production capacity. From an economic point of view, a decrease in the price of oil decreases the willingness of suppliers to produce and sell oil. The *IEO 2005*, however, shows the opposite effect for OPEC countries. One possible explanation is that OPEC countries control the price of oil with their quotas.

The shift toward high oil prices could sharply reduce the growth in future demand for oil, and it could lead to major new investment in all forms of energy supply, conservation, and efficiency. In the interim, however, the following production and resource risks are affecting the efforts of oil-producing nations to expand spare production capacity:

- *Little "sustainable" spare capacity:* With the exception of Saudi Arabia, in 2005 the rest of the world had no spare capacity. If there were sudden surges in demand (caused by high economic growth) or disruption in the supply of other exporters (as by the Iraq war in 2003 and strikes in Venezuela in 2002), would producers be able to meet the shortages that would result? Little analysis exists on the ability to restore meaningful levels of surplus capacity during periods of high demand or on their effects.

- *Elasticity in importer conservation, efficiency, and alternative supply and time/uncertainty lags:* One of the flaws in the current forecasts by the EIA, IEA, and OPEC is that they do not take into account changes in the elasticity of supply and demand. Long-term and midterm elasticities have an impact on the demand, supply, and price, which in turns changes investment incentives and production capacity.

- *Producibililty at given prices:* Some experts have argued that the "easy oil" era is over. Oil recovery is more costly, and the price of oil has to be high enough to cover variable, fixed, and sunk costs and investment, but not so high that it exerts downward pressure on demand. Analysis and modeling need to be updated to reflect more realistic cost assumptions and estimates of the impact of given prices on actual production.

- *Technological gains in the upstream and downstream sector:* Current production capacity forecasts do not and may not be able to anticipate technological gains in the upstream side of the industry, especially demand-driven models. Producers strive to improve efficiency by investing in research and development and new technological innovations, but it remains uncertain how much, how, and when these technological gains may bear fruits in real-world changes in the level of recovery.

- *The "sustainable" inflow of domestic and foreign investment:* Natural depletion of current oil fields is inevitable. Expansion programs, therefore, are needed to replenish this natural decline, but developing countries are in need of domestic foreign investment, including both capital and technological sharing. The lack of security and stability, rigid foreign investment and tax laws, and limited transparency have prevented the inflow of much needed foreign investment into developing countries.

Estimates of near-term spare oil production and export capacity are increasingly uncertain and inevitably differ. According to the IEA, in early 2005 OPEC had spare capacity of 1.92 to 2.42 mmbpd; but according to the EIA, it had 1.1 to 1.6 mmbpd. In both cases, practically all the spare capacity was from Saudi Arabia. The consulting firm HET-CO forecast that OPEC would increase its production by 0.70 mmbpd in 2005. Most of the increase would depend on Saudi Arabia's ability to increase its capacity. HETCO forecast an increase in Saudi production capacity from 10.68 to 11.15 mmbpd.[4] There is almost no way, however, to look much beyond 2005 to predict that there will be relatively stable sources of surplus production capacity in the middle to long terms, or that any combination of nations will maintain the equivalent of 2.0 mmbpd that Saudi Arabia maintained in the past.

SOLVING SUPPLY ISSUES RELATED TO MIDDLE EASTERN OIL

The potential impact of high oil prices in easing the strain on world oil supplies becomes clearer when one looks at the impact of oil prices on the need for Middle Eastern and North African conventional oil production capacity:

- The *IEO 2004* called for major increases in Middle Eastern and North African oil production capacity. It called for a Gulf production capacity in 2025 of 56.80 mmbpd for its low-price case, 45.00 mmbpd for its reference case, and 32.90 mmbpd for its high-price case.

- The *IEO 2005* forecasts that conventional Gulf production capacity in 2025 will be 50.0 mmbpd for the low-price case, 39.30 mmbpd for the reference case, and only 27.80 mmbpd for the high-price case.

For many years, most of OPEC's projected increase in production capacity in both the EIA and IEA models has been driven by Saudi Arabia. Some analysts have questioned the Kingdom's ability to meet sudden surges in demand because of its lack of spare production capacity; others—like Matthew Simmons—have estimated that Saudi production may be moving toward a period of sustained decline.

In 2002, Saudi Arabia had an oil production capacity of 9.2 mmbpd. This capacity was roughly 9.0 to 10.5 mmbpd in 2004 and averaged

10.5–11 mmbpd in 2005. Like most of its predecessors, the *IEO* analysis for 2004 called for truly massive increases in Saudi oil. It forecast that Saudi Arabia's production capacity in 2025 would be 31.5 mmbpd for the low-price case, 22.5 mmbpd for the reference case, and 16.0 mmbpd for the high-price case.

In contrast, the *IEO 2005* forecasts that Saudi Arabia's production capacity in 2025 will be 20.4 mmbpd for the low-price case, 16.3 mmbpd for the reference case, but only 11.0 mmbpd for the high-price case. Yet, Saudi Arabia already plans to increase its production capacity to 12.5 mmbpd by 2009.

Most analysts, including current and former Saudi Aramco officials, believe that even 20.4 mmbpd is an unattainable production capacity for Saudi Arabia and that the practical limit may be closer to between 15.0 and 16.0 mmbpd. At this point, one can argue that the Kingdom could reach this production capacity only if two things happen: (1) major technological breakthroughs enhance the recovery of existing oil fields or help in finding new reservoirs, and (2) major supply disruptions force Saudi Arabia to meet the shortages in supply.

GENERAL PATTERNS OF OIL DEPENDENCE

The United States and China are key "drivers" in the increasing demand for energy imports and production capacity forecast in most models.

U.S. Import Dependence

The United States has become progressively more dependent on both a growing volume of imports and steadily growing imports from troubled countries and regions. Direct U.S. petroleum imports increased from an annual average of 6.3 mmbpd in 1973 to 7.9 in 1992 to 11.3 in 2002 to 12.9 in 2004.

Some 2.5 mmbpd worth of U.S. petroleum imports came directly from the Middle East in 2004.[5] Additionally, the average U.S. petroleum imports from the Persian Gulf alone equaled 2.3 mmbpd in the first six months of 2005, 2.4 in 2004, 2.5 in 2003, 2.2 in 2002, 2.7 in 2001, and 2.4 in 2000.[6]

If one looks at OPEC exports as a share of U.S. imports, these ranged from 47.8 percent of mmbpd in 1973 to 51.9 percent in 1992 to 39.9 percent in 2002 to 43.6 percent in 2004. If one looks at Gulf exports as a share of U.S. imports, these ranged from 13.6 percent of mmbpd in 1973 to 22.5 percent in 1992 to 19.7 percent in 2002 to 19.3 percent in 2004.

Future U.S. gross petroleum imports will vary sharply according to price. If prices are low ($20.99 a barrel), U.S. imports will rise to 47.86 mmbpd in 2025. If prices are moderate ($30.31 a barrel), U.S. imports are still 43.43 mmbpd. If prices rise to $39.87 a barrel, however, U.S. imports are projected to be only 38.87 mmbpd, and they would be far lower at $50, $60, $70, or more per barrel. Even the "high-price" case leaves the United States with nearly 60 percent dependence on oil imports in 2025, but the impact of this dependence on world supply is far lower than if oil prices are low or moderate.

The EIA estimates of future U.S. imports indicate that moderate oil prices will lead to major increases in U.S. imports from the Gulf (from 2.5 mmbpd in 2000 to 6.0 in 2025), the Americas (from 3.1 mmbpd in 2000 to 5.0 in 2025), and "others," including North Africa (from 2.7 mmbpd in 2000 to 6.2 in 2025).

The size of direct U.S. imports of petroleum is only a partial measure of the United States' strategic dependence on imports. The U.S. economy is dependent on energy-intensive imports from Asia and other regions. The failure of the U.S. Department of Energy and the EIA to explicitly model such indirect imports and their steady growth is a long-standing and critical failure in U.S. energy analysis and policy. It seems almost certain that the future increase in such indirect imports will, for example, vastly exceed any benefits in increased domestic energy supply resulting from the energy bill passed by the U.S. Congress in the summer of 2005.

The Surge in Chinese Demand for Oil

China's domestic production could reach 3.8 mmbpd in 2020, but its total national demand is then likely to be more than three times as high.[7] Some experts believe that recent high oil prices can provide the right incentives for investment in new technologies to enhance recovery and exploration and increase China's domestic output, reducing its reliance on oil imports.[8] Nevertheless, during 2004 China imported 40 percent of its oil consumption, despite the fact that it produced 174 million tons of oil during that year. Chapter 4 discusses China's oil imports in detail.

Other Importers

Current models project that African and Middle Eastern imports could double by 2025. India could also be a key factor driving the demand for the growth in global oil exports. Oil makes up 30 percent of India's energy consumption, but the country has only 5.4 billion barrels of oil.[9] In 2001, India consumed 2.1 mmbpd; and in 2003, 2.2. According to the EIA's reference-case forecast, Indian consumption will reach 2.67 mmbpd in 2010 and will double to as high as 4.9 mmbpd in 2025.[10]

Other Asian states could also emerge as major new importers. Russia could increase domestic consumption sharply in ways that would reduce its exports. Western Europe and Japan are the only major importers not projected to massively increase potential demand. Once again, as the following chapters will make clear, the failure to model the high prices, or to examine supply by supplier nations in credible terms, leaves massive uncertainties.

Notes

[1] U.S. Energy Information Administration (EIA), *Monthly Energy Review*, March 2005, 149.

[2] Edward Morse and Thomas Stenvoll, "The New Supplier(s) of Last Resort," *Weekly Market Review*, Hess Energy Trading Company, April 1, 2005.

[3] EIA, *International Energy Outlook 2005*, 26.

[4] Morse and Stenvoll, "New Supplier(s) of Last Resort."

[5] BP, *Statistical Review of World Energy 2005*, June 2003, 17.

[6] EIA, "Petroleum Imports from Qatar, Saudi Arabia, U.A.E. and Total Persian Gulf," *Monthly Energy Review*, August 2005.

[7] Jin Liangziang, "Energy First: China and the Middle East," *Middle East Quarterly*, Spring 2005, available at http://www.meforum.org/article/694.

[8] "China to Control Its Reliance on Oil Imports," *Xinhua*, April 23, 2005, available at http://www2.chinadaily.com.cn/english/doc/2005-04/23/content _436862.htm#.

[9] EIA, Country Analysis Brief, "India," available at http://www.eia.doe.gov/ emeu/cabs/india.html.

[10] EIA, *International Energy Outlook 2005.*

CHAPTER TWO

THE FORCES SHAPING THE GLOBAL ENERGY MARKET

The dynamics of the current oil market involve four major interdependent areas of uncertainty: geostrategic risks, macroeconomic fluctuations, the nature of resource risks, and the uncertainty of current and future oil production capacity.

It is clear that the global energy market is intricate and the analysis of it is uncertain. The ability of policy planners and strategists in petroleum-consuming nations is limited at best. Most of the world's known oil reserves exist in regions and countries that are not stable. Consumers cannot control where reserves exist, and the geostrategic risks are not likely to change in the near future.

At this point, about all that is certain about the forces shaping the world's energy supply is that the global energy market is unpredictable and that recent oil prices have been high and volatile. In four years, the price per barrel of oil has increased by roughly 108 percent. The price of crude oil averaged $25.9 per barrel in 2001; and for the first eight months of 2005, this price increased to approximately $54.1 per barrel.[1]

The geostrategic risks are all too clear. The stability of key petroleum-exporting countries is often tenuous. Algeria, Iran, and Iraq all present immediate security problems, and recent experience has shown that exporting countries in Africa, the Caspian Sea region, and South America are no more stable than those in the Middle East. There have been pipeline sabotage in Nigeria, labor strikes in Venezuela, alleged corruption in Russia, and civil unrest in Uzbekistan and other former Soviet Union states.

Many experts believe that, in the near future, energy supply and transportation routes may be challenged by transnational terrorism and proliferation. It is equally possible, however, that recent surges in the demand for oil, the U.S. refining capacity bottleneck, and limited spare production capacity will continue to test the energy market in the mid to long terms.[2]

Natural disasters, such as hurricanes, earthquakes, and tsunamis, may also prove to be troublesome to the stability of the energy markets by causing production, transportation, and refining disruptions.

These pressures and uncertainties add to the economic risk premium, causing oil prices to rise further. Moreover, though higher oil prices may provide incentives for private and public investment in the oil industry, a lack of geopolitical stability and an inability to predict how long high oil prices will last will continue to prevent many from investing in these areas.

Given the strategic risks faced by oil-producing nations, claims about production goals and capacity and oil reserves have become a political tool. Some producers have inflated their "proven" reserves to project strategic importance, which has again added to the uncertainty and the lack of transparency affecting the understanding of the probable trends in global oil supply.

The fall of the shah of Iran in 1979 and the Iran-Iraq War, for example, led to a competition in the Gulf to announce new levels of "proven" reserves to demonstrate the strategic importance of given countries. The result was major increases in the claims made by Iran, Iraq, Saudi Arabia, Kuwait, and other countries whose validity and comparability are sometimes uncertain.

Limited hard data are available to validate many national claims and plans. In many cases, it is not clear that the U.S. Energy Information Administration (EIA), International Energy Agency (IEA), Organization of the Petroleum Exporting Countries (OPEC), and U.S. Geological Survey (USGS) have applied sufficient rigor to a country-by-country reexamination of such estimates. (The USGS does use a different methodology because it looks at the geological potential basis, but the data available are uncertain and dated.)

THE SHORT-TERM OUTLOOK

In the short run, much depends on just how much pressure demand puts on limited supply, and the resulting impact on oil prices. One paradox is that over a longer period, only high prices bring demand back into balance with the future level of supply. Only a cutback in global economic growth and demand for oil can produce rapid cuts in oil prices, but only high prices can stimulate rapid efforts to increase supply, find alternative sources of supply, and encourage conservation and efficiency.

The modeling of sustained high-price cases is just beginning, but previous modeling efforts provide important insights into what *may* happen. If oil prices drop back to the level of between $31 and $35 a barrel (in 2003 dollars), as assumed in the reference case of the *International Energy Outlook 2005*, the EIA estimates that world demand for oil will increase from 78.0 million barrels per day (mmbpd) in 2002 to 119 mmbpd in 2025. This projected increase in world oil demand would require global oil production to increase by 42.0 mmbpd over the world's 2002 capacity levels—accounting for approximately 38 percent of the world's energy consumption through 2025.[3] In addition, a 2004 EIA report estimates that the United States and its major trading partners in developing Asia will account for 60 percent of the increase in world demand throughout this period.[4]

If oil prices stay at $56 per barrel or above, however, the EIA assumes that major reductions will take place in the rate of increase in U.S. and other global imports. This will not reduce U.S. strategic dependence on imports in the near term but merely slow the rate of increase in dependence. In the long term, the United States and other importers can and must find substitutes for Middle Eastern and North African petroleum, but this will take decades. In the interim, the United States and the global economy will actually become steadily more dependent on energy imports, particularly from the Gulf. Even after adjusting the forecast for high sustained oil prices, members of OPEC, dominated by Gulf state producers, are expected to supply 60 percent of the increased capacity required to meet future world demand.

It is too soon to draw any firm conclusions about the impact of high oil prices on global oil dependence, on U.S. and other imports, and on increases in conservation and the supply of alternative fuels. But these factors indicate that high prices are not necessarily bad for the global economy and could trigger market forces that offset their short-term negative effects. The fact is, however, that no one really knows. Moreover, even if one could guess correctly about the complex mix of elasticities involved, meaningful modeling and analysis are only beginning.

Oil-producing countries are only beginning to reexamine their long-term energy export capacity, investment strategies, and plans. Importing countries are equally slow to announce changes in national policy, and the private sector is only beginning to seriously react to what may or may not be significant shifts in long-term energy prices and the viability of alternative investments.

INADEQUATE MODELING BASED ON INADEQUATE UNDERSTANDING

The key modelers of global energy supply and demand have not yet reacted to the recent rises in oil prices and examined in full detail those cases that go above $50 a barrel. There have been some preliminary efforts by the International Monetary Fund and the EIA in its *International Energy Outlook 2005*. However, the projections by OPEC, the IEA, and the EIA still need to be revised or expanded to fully examine such cases and to examine the implications of a world with a "sustained" price of $60, $80, or even $100 per barrel of oil.

More generally, many laypeople do not understand the wide range of problems with the foundations on which forecasting methodology is based. It is all too clear that the modeling the EIA, IEA, and OPEC have used in forecasting global petroleum supply and demand has been driven by estimating global demand at comparatively low oil prices.

Reports such as the International Energy Outlook 2005 provide important insights into planning, but they do not provide a solid basis for energy analysis in today's world. Reports by the EIA, IEA, and OPEC could provide a better benchmark for the global energy market if they addressed deficiencies. The key gaps and areas of uncertainty in such reports include:

- *Parametric analysis:* A full range of parametric analysis is lacking in energy models and forecasts. Furthermore, models such as the *International Energy Outlook* treat major shifts in energy costs and different levels of economic growth largely as independent assumptions and variables.

- *Economic growth rates:* Models do not reflect sufficient explorations of how the rates of economic growth interact with the price of oil and how the price elasticity of demand changes over time given a particular economic growth rate.

- *Country plans:* Models normally do not take into account country-by-country plans in forecasting oil production capacity. When they do, there is little explanation of how such plans have changed since their last forecast and how realistic or unrealistic those plans are. Analyses of plans to improve downstream production and export capability receive only moderate mentions. National plans for energy security, reserves, redundancy, and repair capability are not considered.

- *Indirect imports:* Models and reports on oil and gas exports do not estimate indirect imports of oil or petroleum from other regions in terms of the energy required to produce finished goods. The United States, for example, indirectly imported very significant amounts of oil in the form of manufactured goods from Asian countries dependent on Middle Eastern oil imports.

- *Technological improvements:* Models do not explicitly analyze the impact of technological improvements in national oil and gas production and export capacity, and the role of technological breakthroughs in enhancing oil recovery and exploration for new oil reservoirs—developments that significantly affect future oil supply and the oil market.

- *Relation of oil prices to demand for alternatives and conservation:* There is little transparency in showing the interactions between different oil prices and the level of oil supply and demand, or changes in the supply of and demand for gas, coal, nuclear power, renewables, electricity, and conservation.

- *Supply and demand elasticities:* Little effort is made to explain, justify, and parametrically model the very different patterns of elasticity in supply of and demand for gas, coal, nuclear power, renewables, electricity, and conservation that have to emerge over time if oil prices remain so much higher than in the past, or the major uncertainties that will inevitably result from such changes.

- *Discontinuity theory:* Models and forecasts use smooth curves and largely "static" assumptions. Growth in demand and supply tends to be at constant rates or in predictable curves. Reality never produces consistent trends or allows trees to grow to the sky. There is a clear need for an assessment of what kinds of sudden events or discontinuities are critical and for some form of Bayesian approach to risk analysis.

As a result of these gaps, the current forecasts of the EIA, IEA, and OPEC tend to illustrate what might happen in a world where virtually everything goes right from the importer's view, where export capacities automatically respond to need, and where political and military risk have no impact.

The costs of new production in the Middle East and North Africa are generally assumed to be extraordinarily low, and there is no explicit analysis of the capability of Saudi Arabia or any other major exporter and supplier to actually produce the amount of oil estimated in the model.

Much of the modeling effort also is based on assumptions and elasticities, which are little more than "guesstimates." The cost factors, and investment estimates for increased production, often seem to be based on cost-analysis methods and data that can be up to 10 or 20 years old and that ignore the needs to develop far more advanced production technology, export from smaller fields, and provide modern infrastructure.

LAGGING INVESTMENT

It is unclear that major exporters have ever or will ever plan to provide the production capacity called for in the low- and moderate-price cases used in past demand-driven models. The IEA *World Energy Outlook 2004* defended such estimates by arguing as follows:

> Fossil-fuel resources are of course, finite, but we are far from exhausting them. The world is not running out of oil just yet. Most estimates of proven oil reserves are high enough to meet the cumulative world demand we project over the next three decades. Our analyses suggest that global production of conventional oil will not peak before 2030 if the necessary investments are made.[5]

Investment in the oil market is dependent on both the health of the global economy and perceptions of future oil prices. Demand is driven by a growth in income and the availability of investment capital. Moreover, aging infrastructure and declining production capacities require funds and new technologies to revive current facilities and build new ones to meet global demand growth.

Providing the kind of massive surges in the demand for oil projected in recent studies between 2005 and 2025 will require massive investments to build new infrastructure and finance new technologies. In 2003, for example, the IEA projected that world oil demand would rise by 60 percent by 2030, and that the world energy market would need $16 trillion in cumulative investment between 2003 and 2030, or $568 billion a year. Even these costs were based on unrealistically low estimates of investment costs and outdated assumptions about the need for the sophisticated exploration, development, and production technology and equipment needed in modern oil fields. Yet they still require vast transfers of capital.

The IEA argues that this is possible, but it qualifies its assessment by saying that "the global financial system has the capacity to fund the required investments, but it will not do so until conditions are right."[6] This is questionable in investment as well as in technical terms.

Moreover, it is unclear whether investment will be an issue unless oil-exporting countries adopt very different plans from those they have so far announced. Key suppliers like Saudi Arabia have never indicated that they will attempt to provide the high levels of production capacity and exports called for in the demand-driven models used by the EIA and the IEA.

The real issue is not investment per se but the massive gap between the goals set by importers and the real-world plans and goals of actual suppliers. This failure to explicitly model real-world supply by country cripples the forecasting efforts of agencies like the EIA and IEA and creates serious doubt as to the forecasts' value at any level of estimated oil prices.

Notes

1. West Texas Intermediate crude oil spot price, adapted from the U.S. Energy Information Administration (EIA) historical database, available at http://www.eia.doe.gov/oil_gas/petroleum/info_glance/prices.html.

2. John J. Fialka, "Search for Crude Comes with New Dangers," *Wall Street Journal*, April 11, 2005.

3. EIA, *International Energy Outlook 2005*, July 2005, 2–3.

4. See http://www.eia.doe.gov/emeu/cabs/pgulf.html. The U.S. Department of Energy / EIA estimated in September 2004 that the Persian Gulf contains 715 billion barrels of proven oil reserves, representing over half (57 percent) of the world's oil reserves, and 2,462 trillion cubic feet of natural gas reserves (45 percent of the world total). In addition, at the end of 2003, Persian Gulf countries maintained about 22.9 mmbpd of oil production capacity, or 32 percent of the world total. Perhaps even more significantly, the Persian Gulf countries normally maintain almost all of the world's excess oil production capacity. As of early September 2004, excess world oil production capacity was only about 0.5 to 1.0 mmbpd, all of which was located in Saudi Arabia.

According to the EIA's *International Energy Outlook 2005* reference-case forecast, Persian Gulf oil production increased from 18.7 mmbpd in 1990 to 22.4 in 2001 to 20.7 in 2002. It is expected to reach about 28.3 mmbpd by 2010, 35.2 in 2020, and 39.3 in 2025. The estimate, however, does change in the high-oil-price case: it is expected to reach about 24.4 mmbpd in 2010, 26.2 in 2020, and 27.8 in 2025.

5. IEA, *World Energy Outlook 2004*, October 2004, 29.

6. IEA, *World Energy Outlook 2004*, Executive Summary, 30.

CHAPTER THREE

RECENT MACROECONOMIC DEVELOPMENTS

Price is a key uncertainty that affects both global demand and the willingness of oil-producing states to fund new capacity and boost their production. Until recently, prices were low enough that little examination was made of the macroeconomics of high oil prices. Through 2004, the U.S. Energy Information Administration (EIA), the International Energy Agency (IEA), and the Organization of the Petroleum Exporting Countries (OPEC) still projected low-price cases of $17 a barrel of oil, reference cases of $27 a barrel, and high-price cases of no more than $35 a barrel.

In 2005, the EIA did adjust its price forecasts to take into account higher oil prices, with $21 a barrel for the low-price case, $35 a barrel for the reference case, and $48 a barrel for the high-price case. This price range of $21 to $48 a barrel still seems too low, however, given recent developments in the global energy market. For example, the *International Energy Outlook 2005* forecast that the price per barrel would increase by $11 in 2005. After Hurricane Katrina hit the U.S. Gulf Coast, the price per barrel reached $70.

In early 2005, the Saudi oil minister, Ali Al-Naimi, stated that he expected oil prices to stay between $40 and $50 a barrel for the rest of 2005. By the end of August 2005, the price had actually surpassed $70 per barrel. The OPEC secretary general stated that the price of a barrel might reach $80, and Goldman Sachs stated that the price could be between $50 and $105.

The key question for future oil supply and demand is whether such price levels will represent the average price band over time. A serious recession in a key importer like the United States, China, or the European Union could change the situation, and there are many other uncertainties. Some energy experts question whether the latest oil price hikes are due to conventional supply/demand forces or to a "bubble." Lee R. Raymond, the chairman and chief executive of ExxonMobil, said, "We are in the mode where the fundamentals of supply and demand really don't drive the price. . . . Oil is a commodity, and history tells us the commodity prices never stay high forever."[1] Some experts holding this view see today's prices as a supply/demand phenomenon and that oil prices are high because the market forces *believed* that OPEC would not be able to clear the market in the fourth quarter of 2004.[2]

Other experts take a different stand. They believe that recent high oil prices have been due to steadily rising demand for oil mixed with production limits driven by factors like high depletion rates of oil fields. The consulting firm CIBC predicts that oil prices will average $77 per barrel and could reach as high as $100 during the period 2005–2010.[3]

THE UNCERTAINTIES DRIVING MODELING AND FORECASTING

Like all economic forecasts, predicting supply, demand, and prices of crude oil involves significant uncertainty. The following key factors influence the oil market, and each involves major uncertainties and unknowns:

- *The geopolitics, security, and stability of oil-exporting nations:* As mentioned above, the Gulf contains more than 65 percent of the world's proven reserves. Stability in these countries, and the security of oil fields and routes of transportation in the region, are of paramount importance to the oil market.

- *The sustainable and spare capacity of oil-producing countries:* In recent years, there has been much debate about the spare capacity of OPEC nations and their ability to "balance the market." In this case, perceptions are as important as realities. The market's lack of confidence in oil producers to meet demand adds a risk premium to any estimates and pushes prices up.

- *The cost of sustaining and expanding petroleum production and exports, and of the necessary investments:* Most of today's estimates of the cost of future production are badly dated and do not take into account the cost of the most advanced technology for exploration, development, and production, or the scale of the investment needed in distribution in areas like port facilities, new tankers, and refineries. Cost models need major reevaluation.

- *Country capability and practice in sustaining and expanding oil production and exports:* There has been little effort to assess country-by-country capability to use best practices and to adopt the most advanced technology and methods. Countries like Kuwait and Iran have failed to move forward in using such practices for very different reasons. Countries like Iraq face insurgency, the risk of civil war, and a long legacy of underfunding proper development.

- *The long-term elasticity of supply and demand:* The development of alternative sources of energy or conservation could have long-term effects on the market, but time lags, investment costs, and delivery prices are uncertain at best in the near future. This inevitably compounds the problem of estimating the elasticity of demand for oil and gas exports.

- *The refining capacity and inventory buildup of the importing nations:* The lack of ability of importing and exporting states to refine crude oil and distribute it to the domestic market in a timely manner can create bottlenecks that not only squeeze the average consumer but also have a negative impact on demand by driving up the price of crude futures because of a product-driven market. Gas ports, pipelines, and distribution system constraints have an equal impact on gas supply.

- *Security problems and accidents:* The world can absorb the problems created by most forms of local conflict and internal security problems when there is significant surplus capacity of energy exports and if prices start from a relatively low base. Behavior changes drastically, however, when supply is very limited and prices are already high. Even potential threats to petroleum production, exports, and distribution can radically alter prices and market behavior. Actual attacks, or major industrial accidents, can have a much more serious impact. The loss of a major supplier, or a sustained major reduction in regional exports, potentially can have unpredictable price and supply effects that have a negative impact on the entire global economy.

- *Natural disasters:* Natural incidents in producing, exporting, or refining areas can be damaging to the energy market. Hurricanes in the Gulf of Mexico have caused supply and distribution disruptions in the United States, and they have added large premiums to the price of a barrel of oil. Hurricanes Katrina and Rita, which hit the U.S. Gulf Coast during August and September 2005, shut down most of the refineries in the U.S. Gulf of Mexico and forced the United States to release some of its strategic petroleum reserves. They also had a major impact on domestic gas production and prices, and the need for imports.

- *Security of supply:* There are few explicit data and little analysis on what exporting countries are doing to help secure their production and export facilities. The size and quality of security and paramilitary forces are often unknown. The quality of repair capability, redundancy, emergency response, and recovery plans is largely unknown. Little analysis exists of the security of ports, offshore facilities, tanker routes, and other critical infrastructure. The analysis of vulnerability to terrorism and attack has been limited at best.

- *The overall health of the global economy:* Economic growth rates in developed countries vary in predictable ways with the price of a barrel of oil. High world oil prices slow the economic growth of consuming nations, and low economic growth in industrialized nations causes a decrease in demand for oil and eventually lowers oil prices. The elasticities and relationships involved, however, are far more uncertain than in the past. It is also very difficult to model the real-world behavior in most countries and regions involved in finding alternative sources of energy, adopting better approaches to conservation, and increasing energy efficiency. This uncertainty becomes progressively greater with time.

- *The rise of China and India:* In recent years, the global oil market has experienced an increased demand from countries in Asia such as China and India. In 2004, emerging economies accounted for nearly 1.9 million barrels per day (mmbpd) of the 2.7 mmbpd increase in world consumption. More than half of the 1.9 mmbpd increase is solely attributable to China. According to the EIA *International Energy Outlook 2005*, the demand from emerging Asia will more than double by 2025.[4]

- *The true size of import dependence:* Current estimates of import dependence only include direct petroleum imports. They do not reflect indirect imports in terms of the energy required to produce manufactured goods. In some critical cases, like the United States, this grossly understates the true nature of import dependence. The United States has become steadily more dependent on Asian manufactured goods, which require Asia to import petroleum, largely from the Middle East. As a result, much of China's increase in import dependence is actually to meet the demands of the United States and other Western markets.

- *Problems in import-dependent developing countries:* Countries with relatively free market economies that are highly developed are rich and flexible enough to adapt to high prices and supply problems far more flexibly than poor countries, countries with serious foreign reserve and balance-of-payments problems, and importers with high levels of subsidies for oil and gas. By and large, the impact of high prices is not modeled in such terms.

- *The cost and economic impact of energy interruptions:* A review of current estimates of the economic impact of interruptions in energy imports indicates they are based on assumptions and models that are badly outdated, do not reflect current prices, and do not reflect cases where the market had already largely exhausted surplus oil production capacity. Such models badly need updating.

- *Problems in refining capacity and energy distribution:* Current models generally consider only total petroleum consumption and do not analyze the problems created by limited refinery capacity and dependence on given types of crude. They do not distinguish adequately between heavy and light oil or sweet and sour crude, do not consider loss of refinery capacity, and do not reflect the limits in the ability of existing refinery capacity to provide given types of product. Little parametric or risk analysis has been done of whether or not estimated rates of refinery construction and gain are possible.

- *Discontinuity theory:* Models and forecasts use smooth curves and largely "static" assumptions. Growth in demand and supply tends to be at constant rates or in predictable curves. Reality never produces consistent trends or allows trees to grow to the sky. There is a clear need for an assessment of what kinds of sudden events or discontinuities are critical and for some form of Bayesian approach to risk analysis.

These are important risks and uncertainties that energy forecasters and policy planners have to take into account. One aspect of energy policy that can be forecast is that policymakers need both an explicit understanding of the uncertainties they face and also every analytic aid they can get in making the right decisions.

FACTORS SHAPING SUPPLY AND DEMAND

Most current short-term forecasts project a relatively high level of average demand through the end of their forecast period. The IEA *World Energy Outlook 2004* summarized regional macroeconomic developments in the energy market as follows:[5]

- Primary energy demand in countries belonging to the Organization for Economic Cooperation and Development (OECD) is projected to grow by 0.9 percent a year over the projection period. It will be almost a third higher in 2030 than it is today. The shares of natural gas and nonhydroelectric renewables will increase at the expense of coal, oil, and nuclear power. The OECD's share of global energy use will continue to fall, from 52 percent in 2002 to 43 percent in 2030.

- Among OECD regions, North America and Oceania will experience the fastest growth in energy demand. OECD Asia demand will grow slightly less quickly, with robust growth in South Korea balancing sluggish demand in Japan. OECD Europe will see the lowest rate of demand growth.

- Total primary energy demand in developing countries as a whole is projected to rise by 2.6 percent a year over the period 2002–2030. Developing countries will account for about two-thirds of the increase in world energy demand. Their share of world energy demand will rise from 37 percent today to nearly half in 2030.

- China will be responsible for 21 percent of the increase in world energy demand to 2030. Coal will continue to be the dominant fuel in China, but the shares of oil, natural gas, and nuclear energy in the primary fuel mix will grow. By 2030, Chinese oil imports will equal the imports of the United States today. China will account for 26 percent of the world's incremental carbon dioxide emissions from now to 2030.

- India's primary energy demand will increase by 2.3 percent, reaching 1,026 million tons oil equivalent by 2030. Biomass and waste, the main fuels in the primary energy mix today, will be increasingly displaced by coal and oil. Brazil's energy demand will grow at an annual average rate of 2.5 percent from now to 2030. Oil and renewables are expected to remain the key fuels in its energy mix. Gas will make major inroads in power generation, particularly toward the end of the projection period.

- The amount of energy that each person consumes will continue to vary widely across regions. Even in 2030, per capita energy use in Africa and South Asia will be less than 15 percent of that in the OECD countries. The transition to modern fuels is expected to continue in developing countries, but Africa and large parts of Asia will remain heavily dependent on biomass.

More recent forecasts generally agree with these points, although they recognize that oil prices are volatile and are shaped by many interdependent factors.

The Factors That Could Sustain High Demand

The short-term trends in demand clearly push against the limits of global supply. According to the U.S. Department of Energy, world oil demand will exceed 86.0 mmbpd in the fourth quarter of 2005, which represents an increase of 1.6 to 1.9 mmbpd. Furthermore, demand is projected to increase by 1.8 to 2.1 mmbpd over the entire year.[6]

The industrialized world and the United States help drive this growth in demand. In 2004, world oil demand increased by 2.7 mmbpd, and according to the head of the EIA, a third of the increase was due to an increase in Chinese demand for oil.[7] In 2004, the United States consumed 20.7 mmbpd; China, 6.5; Japan, 5.4; Germany, 2.6; Russia, 2.3; Canada, 2.3; India, 2.3; and South Korea, 2.1.[8]

The oil consumption of the OECD countries in 2004 was 48.8 mmbpd, 5.2 percent higher than in 2003. The changes in consumption were as follows: United Kingdom, +2.4 percent; Germany, –1.2 percent; Canada, +3.9 percent; France, +0.9 percent; United States, +2.8 percent; Italy, –2.8 percent; Japan, –3.0 percent; and South Korea, –0.8 percent.[9]

World demand for oil in 2002 was 78.20 mmbpd, and for the first quarter of 2005 it reached 84.18 mmbpd. The EIA estimated that for the first quarter of 2005, the United States consumed 20.63 mmbpd; China, 6.83; Japan, 6.05; Germany, 2.52; Canada, 2.35; South Korea, 2.40; and the rest of Asia, 8.17.[10]

The International Monetary Fund forecasts a sharp increase in global demand for crude oil from emerging economies in Asia. It projects that the world oil demand growth rate will be 2.1 mmbpd every year. Due to this surge, the IMF forecasts that the price per barrel of oil will be $34 in 2010 and between $39 and $56 in 2030. It concludes that the world needs to adapt to high oil prices for the next 20 years and that the global economy faces "permanent oil shock."[11]

Moreover, the *International Energy Outlook 2005* projects that high levels of growth in key emerging economies, particularly those in Asia such as India and China, will account for much of the increase in the global demand for oil, which the EIA projects will grow at 3.5 percent a year over the next 20 years. This growth in the demand for oil is directly

linked, however, to robust economic conditions in emerging economies such as China and India. Transitional economies such as those in
Eastern Europe and the former Soviet Union (FSU) will witness an oil
demand growth of 1.4 percent a year, which translates into an increase
in their oil consumption from 5.5 mmbpd in 2002 to 7.6 mmbpd in
2025.[12]

China replaced Japan as the second largest consumer of petroleum
in 2004. During the same year, total Chinese consumption of petroleum products averaged 6.5 mmbpd. The EIA claims that China was
the source of about 40 percent of the global energy demand growth in
2004.

The "China factor" will continue to play a major part in global energy demand. Since 1983, China has been a net importer of oil, and it
will continue to be dependent on foreign oil, namely Middle Eastern
oil, for the foreseeable future. The EIA projected in 2005 that Chinese
consumption could reach 14.2 mmbpd in 2025 and that Chinese imports will reach 10.98 mmbpd of it total petroleum demand (77 percent of its total consumption needs).[13]

The "India factor" is also important in shaping the increase in demand. India in 2001 consumed 2.1 mmbpd; and in 2003, 2.2. Oil already makes up 30 percent of India's energy consumption, but the
country has only 5.4 billion barrels of oil.[14] According to the EIA's reference-case forecast, Indian consumption will reach 2.67 mmbpd in
2010 and double to as high as 4.9 mmbpd in 2025.[15]

Growth seems likely to be much slower in developed Asia, but still is
an important force in the market. Japan consumed 5.3 mmbpd in
1990, 5.4 in 2001, 5.3 in 2002, 5.5 in 2003, and 5.4 in 2004. The lack of
growth in the Japanese demand for oil is also apparent in the EIA forecast. The reference-case forecast of the *International Energy Outlook
2005*, for example, projects that Japan's consumption in 2025 will be
5.3 mmbpd.[16]

Other industrialized nations are projected to have higher growth
rates than Japan, in spite of rising prices. On April 5, 2005, the U.S. Federal Reserve chairman, Alan Greenspan, said, "Higher prices in recent
months have slowed the growth of oil demand, but only modestly."
Greenspan also noted that the high oil prices are due to "geopolitical

uncertainties" in the oil-producing states. He also argued that "the status of world refining capacity has become worrisome," and that these factors are creating a "price frenzy."[17]

Longer-term estimates project high growth rates, although partly because the total world production capacity of oil is assumed to meet the increases in global oil demand. Because the *International Energy Outlook 2005* does not examine the impact of high oil prices on world energy balances, there is no way to guess at how much this would change if oil prices remained high. The numbers above, however, provide a good benchmark for the analysis of global oil demand and supply.

It is also important to note that the total growth for "other Asia" nearly totals the growth in China. Total Asian demand is estimated to rise from 21.5 mmbpd in 2002 to between 35.6 and 45.50 mmbpd in 2025. India's oil demand is estimated to increase from 2.20 mmbpd in 2002 to between 4.30 and 5.40 mmbpd in 2025. Other Asia's oil demand is estimated to rise from 5.6 mmbpd in 2002 to between 9.80 and 13.4 mmbpd in 2025. South Korea's demand for oil is estimated to rise from 2.20 mmbpd in 2002 to between 2.60 and 3.40 mmbpd in 2025.

Figure 3.1 shows the EIA estimates of total world demand for three cases based on different economic growth rates: low, reference, and high. For the low-economic-growth case, the EIA estimates that total world demand will be 98.60 mmbpd in 2010, 110.0 in 2015, 120.60 in 2020, and 132.30 in 2025. For the reference case, total world demand is estimated to be 93.60 mmbpd in 2010, 103.20 in 2015, 111.0 in 2020, and 119.20 in 2025. For the high-economic-growth case, total world demand is expected to reach 91.0 mmbpd in 2010, 97.20 in 2015, 102.30 in 2020, and 107.7 in 2025.

According to these projections, the elasticity of demand becomes steeper with time. Total world demand for oil will drop by 9.6 percent in 2025, compared with 2.6 percent in 2010, if the economic growth rate changes from reference to high; it will rise by 10.9 percent in 2025, compared with 5.3 percent in 2010, if the economic growth rate changes from reference to low; and it will increase by 23.4 percent in 2025, compared with 7.6 percent in 2010, if the economic growth rate changes from low to high.[18]

Figure 3.1
U.S. EIA Estimate of World Demand Based on Economic Growth,
2001–2025 (million barrels per day)

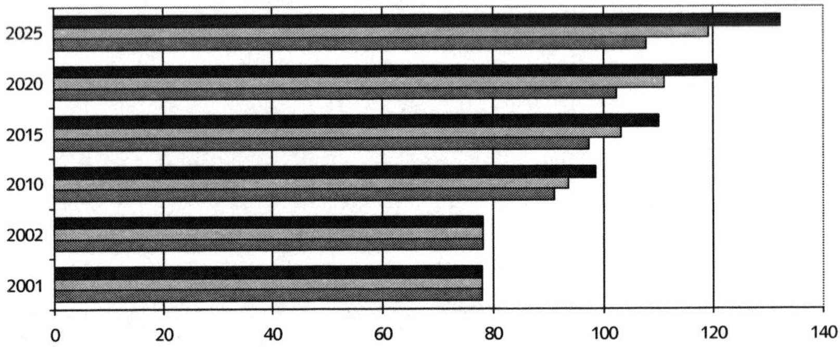

	2001	2002	2010	2015	2020	2025
■ LG	78.00	78.20	98.60	110.00	120.60	132.30
▨ R	78.00	78.20	93.60	103.20	111.00	119.20
▩ HG	78.00	78.20	91.10	97.20	102.30	107.70

Source: Adapted by the authors from U.S. Energy Information Administration,
  International Energy Outlook 2005.
Note: LG = low-growth case; R = reference case; HG = high-growth case

The Forces That Could Shape Limited Supply

If any of these changes in levels of sustained average demand growth
actually occurs, virtually all estimates indicate that it will put a growing strain on both global petroleum supply and export capacity. BP's
Statistical Review of World Energy 2005 reported that in 2004, the average total world production was 80.26 mmbpd—higher than the 2003
average by 3.206 mmbpd.

In 2004, OPEC produced 32.927 mmbpd, which is a 7.7 percent increase from its 2003 production levels of 2.241 mmbpd, Russia increased its production by 0.741 mmbpd (+8.9 percent), and China by
0.089 mmbpd (+2.9 percent).[19]

Non-OPEC supply so far has been slow to respond to the high oil
prices. In fact, it increased by only 0.046 mmbpd in 2004 (31.8 percent
of which came from the FSU). According to the U.S. Department of
Energy, the expected increase in non-OPEC oil production for 2005 is

0.92 mmbpd.[20] In 2005 and 2006, more than half of this non-OPEC increase is estimated to come from the FSU and the Atlantic Basin, including Latin America and West Africa.[21]

Estimates of spare capacity are increasingly uncertain and inevitably differ. According to the IEA, in early 2005, OPEC had spare capacity of 1.92 to 2.42 mmbpd, but according to the EIA, it had 1.1 to 1.6 mmbpd. In both cases, practically all the spare capacity was from Saudi Arabia. The consulting firm HETCO forecast that in 2005, OPEC would increase its production by 0.70 mmbpd. Again, most of the increase will depend on Saudi Arabia's ability to increase its capacity. HETCO forecast an increase in Saudi production capacity of from 10.68 to 11.15 mmbpd.[22]

As for longer-term supply and demand, the EIA forecasts that world production will steadily increase in the next two decades. Its 2005 modeling-efforts estimate marks a slight decrease from the 2004 projections due to the forecasting of a longer period of sustained high oil prices.[23]

In 2002, the world oil production capacity was 80.0 mmbpd. Looking toward the future, figure 3.2 shows the estimates the EIA made in 2005 for world production capacity for the low-price case ($21 a barrel), reference case ($35 a barrel), and high-price case ($48 a barrel):

- For the low-price case, the EIA estimates that total world oil production capacity will be 101.60 mmbpd in 2010, 113.30 in 2015, 123.90 in 2020, and 135.20 in 2025.

- For the reference case, total world production capacity is estimated to be 96.50 mmbpd in 2010, 105.40 in 2015, 113.60 in 2020, and 122.20 in 2025.

- For the high-economic-growth case, total world production is estimated to reach 94.60 mmbpd in 2010, 101.80 in 2015, 108.50 in 2020, and 115.50 in 2025.

As is the case with the elasticity of demand, the elasticity of supply becomes greater with time. Total world oil production capacity will drop by 5.4 percent in 2025, compared with 1.9 percent in 2010, if the price changes from reference to high; it will rise by 10.6 percent in

Figure 3.2
U.S. EIA Estimate of Total World Supply Production Capacity,
2001–2025 (million barrels per day)

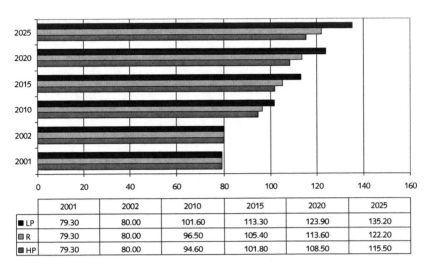

	2001	2002	2010	2015	2020	2025
■ LP	79.30	80.00	101.60	113.30	123.90	135.20
▨ R	79.30	80.00	96.50	105.40	113.60	122.20
▦ HP	79.30	80.00	94.60	101.80	108.50	115.50

Source: Adapted by the authors from U.S. Energy Information Administration,
International Energy Outlook 2005.
Note: Prices are projected to be low-price case (LP = $21); reference case (R = $35); and
high-price case (HP = $48).

2025, compared with 5.2 percent in 2010, if the price changes from reference to low; and it will increase by 14.5 percent in 2025, compared with 6.8 percent in 2010, if the price changes from low to high. In any case, the forecast increases in oil capacity meet the increase in oil demand.[24]

There are, however, many risks and uncertainties on the supply side in both the short and long terms, which such forecasts only partially consider. In the short term, such uncertainties include these types of factors:

- The surge in oil demand has pushed many producing countries to operate at their maximum capacity, which has instilled fears of a lack of spare capacity in case of further spikes in the market.

- Some oil firms have downgraded their reserve estimates for certain oil fields.

- Oman has falling production levels.

- Kuwait and the United Arab Emirates have been slow to modernize production facilities and techniques.

- The world oil market is losing 1.0 mmbpd from depletion every year.[25]

- There is uncertainty about the flow of Iraqi oil exports in the face of the country's high level of internal turmoil and the lack of any technological upgrading of its oil infrastructure since the Gulf War.

- There are continued political uncertainties in Iran and unrealistic policies toward foreign investment by the current Iranian government.

- Much damage was inflicted on the U.S. Gulf Coast and offshore oil installations following Hurricanes Charley, Frances, Ivan, Katrina, and Rita.

- There are capacity constraints (upstream, downstream, and transportation).

- In addition, Venezuelan political instability, Nigerian labor strikes, and internal strife between the Russian government and the giant oil firm Yukos also contributed to pushing crude oil and other petroleum prices higher in 2005.

In the longer-term, such uncertainties include these types of factors:

- The actual level of producible reserves in virtually all developing states at given levels of price and technology. Experts like Matthew Simmons seriously question whether current estimates seriously exaggerate such capability. The EIA's country-by-country analyses indicate that major additional proven reserves await discovery in Saudi Arabia and virtually every Middle Eastern and North African country.

- The real-world cost of incremental production capacity. Current EIA, IEA, and OPEC estimates almost certainly use cost estimates that are too low for Saudi Arabia and other Middle Eastern and North African countries, and that understate the full cost of infrastructure and advanced recovery techniques. What is not clear is what the real cost will be.

- Debates over the commercially recoverable oil in existing oil fields and countries, the sustainability of production with current recovery techniques, and future technology gain.

- The rate of maturity and decline in given oil fields with present and future technology.

- The future commercial potential of tar sands and heavy oil, a factor that could sharply change the distribution of the world's commercial reserves, if resources like Canadian tar sands become as cost-effective as nations like Canada hope.

- Major uncertainties over the ability to find and produce oil beyond the levels counted in proven reserves. BP's 2005 *Statistical Review* estimates that global proven reserves are 1,188.6 billion barrels,[26] while in 2004 the EIA projected that reserve growth will provide another 334.5 billion barrels (a growth rate of 26 percent), and another 538.4 billion barrels are undiscovered (an additional growth rate of 43 percent).[27]

- Long-term substitution effects that bring alternative fuels on line at competitive prices at whatever petroleum price levels emerge over time.

Supply disruptions continue to be a constant risk, and they have contributed to high oil prices in recent years. The global energy market has experienced supply disruptions due to labor strikes, oil infrastructure sabotages, and natural disasters. On April 5, 2002, half the workers at Venezuela's national oil company, PdVSA, went on a strike, causing two out of the five Venezuelan export terminals to stop operating.

Another example is provided by the effect of Hurricanes Ivan, Katrina, and Rita. On September 14, 2004, the companies in the Gulf of Mexico's coast, including Shell, ExxonMobil, ChevronTexaco, and Total, had to shut down their production and evacuate 3,000 of their workers from their offshore platforms. The U.S. Mineral Management Service (MMS) estimated that Ivan caused the Gulf of Mexico's oil production to decline by 61 percent.[28] According to MMS, Hurricane

Katrina caused the Gulf Coast's production to decline by 0.89 mmbpd, which represents roughly 60 percent of its production.[29] The situation is too uncertain to draw any conclusion about the medium- to long-term effects of Hurricane Katrina.

Capacity constraints, and the perception that supply is limited, have also had as much influence as actual supply disruptions. The world energy market will add only 300,000 barrels of net new onstream supply from 2006 to 2010. This lack of growth is estimated to be met by a 2.5 percent increase in demand. Prices would need to rise to clear the market.[30]

All these factors confront the global economy and energy producers with a world where not only are demand-driven capacity and export forecasts unreliable, but where the risks caused by such uncertainties are growing more serious. Forecasts based on low prices have already proven wrong, and this may turn out to be equally true of forecasts that point to relatively "high" oil prices that range from $40 to $105.

If such high prices occur, they will eventually dampen demand for crude oil, and the magnitude of the real-world drop will depend on the elasticity of demand one assumes. Updated forecast models need to be built to adjust for the recent high oil prices and to modify past assumptions about the interdependence between supply forecasts, prices, and current and future demand.

Demand will always be equally unpredictable. Demand may well decrease with a slowdown in Asian growth—"trees do not grow to the sky," even in China and India. If demand does rise steadily, however, oil-producing countries such as Saudi Arabia will face growing challenges in trying to simultaneously increase production to meet demand, replace depleted fields, and recover a reserve of 2.0 mmbpd—which would in any case become a steadily smaller percentage of world demand.

The marginal cost of surplus capacity in a high-demand market could also be extremely high, particularly because the real-world marginal cost of incremental production is rising all around the globe, given increased technical sophistication in production and lower-yield oil fields.

Notes

[1] Sunib Rinerio, "Experts See Bubble in High Oil Prices," *New York Times*, March 15, 2005.

[2] Edward Morse and Thomas Stenvoll, "The New Supplier(s) of Last Resort," *Weekly Market Review*, Hess Energy Trading Company, April 1, 2005.

[3] CIBC, "Monthly Indicators," April 5, 2005; available at http://research .cibcwm.com/res/Eco/ArEcoMI.html.

[4] U.S. Energy Information Administration (EIA), *International Energy Outlook 2005*, July 2005, 26.

[5] IEA, *World Energy Outlook 2004*, October 2004, chap. 18, 243.

[6] Morse and Stenvoll, "New Supplier(s) of Last Resort."

[7] Robert Samuelson, "A New Era for Oil," *Washington Post*, March 30, 2005.

[8] EIA, "Non-OPEC Fact Sheet," June 2005.

[9] EIA, *Monthly Energy Review*, March 2005, 149.

[10] EIA, "World Oil Demand, 2001–2005," *International Petroleum Monthly*, August 2005, table 2.4.

[11] Javier Blas, "IMF Warns on Risk of 'Permanent Oil Shock,'" *Financial Times*, April 7, 2005.

[12] EIA, *International Energy Outlook 2005*, 26.

[13] EIA, Country Analysis Brief, "China," available at http://www.eia.doe .gov/emeu/cabs/china.html.

[14] EIA, Country Analysis Brief, "India," available at http://www.eia.doe .gov/emeu/cabs/india.html.

[15] EIA, *International Energy Outlook 2005*.

[16] Ibid.

[17] Patrice Hill, "Greenspan Calls 'Price Frenzy' for Oil a Concern," *Washington Times*, April 6, 2005.

[18] EIA, *International Energy Outlook 2005*.

[19] EIA, *Monthly Energy Review*, March 2005, 149.

[20] Morse and Stenvoll, "New Supplier(s) of Last Resort."

[21] EIA, *International Energy Outlook 2005*, 26.

[22] Morse and Stenvoll, "New Supplier(s) of Last Resort."

[23] EIA, *International Energy Outlook 2005*, 8.

[24] EIA, *International Energy Outlook 2005*.

[25] CIBC, "Monthly Indicators."

[26] BP, *Statistical Review of World Energy 2005*, June 2005, 4.

[27] EIA, *International Energy Outlook 2004*, June 2004, 36.

[28] EIA, "Chronology of World Oil Market Events 1970–2004," available at http://www.eia.doe.gov/emeu/cabs/chron.html.

[29] EIA, "Hurricane Katrina's Impact on the U.S. Oil and Natural Gas Market," *Special Reports*, September 9, 2005; available at http://tonto.eia.doe.gov/oog/special/eia1_katrina.html.

[30] CIBC, "Monthly Indicators."

CHAPTER FOUR

SHIFTS IN GLOBAL OIL DEPENDENCE

As mentioned earlier in the book, the 2005 forecast by the U.S. Energy Information Administration (EIA) indicates that world consumption will increase steadily in the next 20 years. Total crude oil demand in 2025 would be 119.20 million barrels per day (mmbpd), compared with 78.20 mmbpd in 2002, requiring roughly a 42.0 mmbpd increase in world oil production capacity to meet the increase in demand.

Table 4.1 shows the trends in regional consumption of oil based on three different cases: high, reference, and low. These cases reflect different economic growth rates by each region, and the *International Energy Outlook 2005* divides the world into three major areas based on their economic development: Mature market economies (the United States, Canada, Mexico, Western Europe, Japan, and Australia); transitional economies (the states of the former Soviet Union, or FSU; and Eastern Europe); and emerging economies (China, India, South Korea, other Asia, Brazil, other Central and South America, Africa, and the Middle East).

As has been discussed earlier in the book, these estimates are based on forecasts that China will dominate the growth of consumption for the next two decades—followed by India, other East Asian states, other Middle Eastern states, Africa, and the United States. Japanese oil consumption, conversely, is forecast to plateau. These shifts will occur at a time when the United States and other industrial states are more and more dependent on both the health of the global economy and increasing

Table 4.1
U.S. EIA Estimates of World Consumption by Region, 2002–2025 (million barrels per day)

Country or Region	Total 2002	2010 Low	2010 Ref.	2010 High	2015 Low	2015 Ref.	2015 High	2020 Low	2020 Ref.	2020 High	2025 Low	2025 Ref.	2025 High
Western Europe	13.80	13.70	14.10	14.40	13.80	14.30	14.80	13.80	14.40	15.20	14.10	14.90	15.90
Japan	5.30	5.20	5.30	5.40	5.20	5.40	5.50	5.10	5.40	5.60	5.00	5.30	5.60
Russia	2.60	2.80	3.00	3.10	2.90	3.10	3.30	3.80	3.30	3.60	3.10	3.40	3.90
China	5.20	8.80	9.20	9.60	9.90	10.70	11.40	11.10	12.30	13.50	12.50	14.20	16.10
India	2.20	2.90	3.10	3.20	3.40	3.70	3.90	3.90	4.20	4.60	4.30	4.90	5.40
South Korea	2.20	2.40	2.60	2.70	2.60	2.80	3.00	2.60	2.90	3.20	2.60	2.90	3.40
Other Asia	5.60	7.40	7.90	8.40	8.30	9.20	10.10	9.10	10.40	11.70	9.80	11.60	13.40
Middle East	5.70	6.90	7.30	7.60	7.30	8.00	8.70	7.60	8.60	9.60	7.90	9.20	10.50
Africa	2.70	3.60	3.70	3.90	4.00	4.30	4.60	4.20	4.60	5.10	4.40	4.90	5.50
Canada	2.10	2.30	2.30	2.40	2.40	2.50	2.60	2.50	2.50	2.70	2.50	2.60	2.70
Mexico	2.00	2.20	2.30	2.30	2.40	2.50	2.60	2.60	2.80	2.90	2.80	3.00	2.90
United States	23.80	22.20	22.50	23.80	23.50	24.20	25.80	24.80	25.80	27.90	25.90	27.30	30.00
Australia/New Zealand	1.00	1.20	1.20	1.20	1.20	1.30	1.30	1.30	1.40	1.40	1.40	1.50	1.60
Russia	2.60	2.80	3.00	3.10	2.90	3.10	3.30	3.80	3.30	3.60	3.10	3.40	3.90
Other FSU	1.50	1.70	1.80	1.80	1.70	1.80	2.00	1.80	1.90	2.10	1.80	2.00	2.30
Eastern Europe	1.40	1.60	1.60	1.70	1.70	1.80	1.90	1.80	1.90	2.10	1.80	2.10	2.40
South and Central America	5.20	6.30	6.80	7.20	6.90	7.80	8.40	7.30	8.50	9.30	7.80	9.30	10.40
Total	82.30	91.20	94.70	98.70	97.20	103.40	109.90	103.30	110.90	120.50	107.70	119.10	132.00

Adapted by the authors from U.S. Energy Information Administration, *International Energy Outlook 2005.*
Note: The three cases are high economic growth, low economic growth, and reference-case economic growth.

flows of oil exports to major suppliers outside the industrial world. With the exception of Latin America, Mexico, and Canada, all of the United States' major trading partners are critically dependent on Middle Eastern oil exports.

Even today, the Middle East and North Africa dominate inter-area movements of petroleum, literally "fuel" the exports of Asia to the rest of the world, and are critical sources of indirect energy exports to other regions. As table 4.2 shows, in 2004, the Middle East and North Africa supplied 5.127 of 12.538 mmbpd of European imports (40.9 percent). Middle Eastern and North African exporters supplied 4.202 mmbpd of Japan's total imports of 5.203 mmbpd (80.8 percent). And Middle Eastern and North African countries supplied 1.306 mmbpd of China's total imports of 3.410 mmbpd (38.3 percent and growing steadily in recent years), 0.135 mmbpd of Australasia's total imports of 0.694 mmbpd (19.5 percent), and 7.33 of 9.294 mmbpd in total imports by other Asian and Pacific states (78.9 percent).[1]

GROWING ASIAN-DRIVEN DEMAND FOR MIDDLE EASTERN AND NORTH AFRICAN EXPORTS

The EIA and the International Energy Agency (IEA) project that the global economy will grow far more dependent on the Middle East and North Africa in the future. The EIA *International Energy Outlook 2005* projected that North America's imports of Middle Eastern and North African oil will rise from roughly 3.3 mmbpd in 2004 to 5.8 mmbpd in 2025—an increase of 91 percent, almost all of which will go to the United States. The increase in exports to Western Europe will be from 4.7 to 7.6 mmbpd, rising 62 percent.

This estimate is based on an oil price of $35 a barrel, but it also assumes that there will be major increases in oil exports from the FSU and that conservation will limit the scale of European imports from the Middle East. Industrialized Asia—driven by Japan—will increase its imports from 4.1 to 6.0 mmbpd, or nearly 50 percent; China will increase its imports from 0.9 to 6.0 mmbpd, or nearly 570 percent; and the Pacific Rim states will increase imports from 5.0 to 10.2 mmbpd, or 104 percent.

Table 4.2
BP Estimates of Inter-area Movements, 2004 (million barrels per day)

	U.S.	Canada	Mexico	S&CAm	Europe	Africa	AusA	China	Japan	Other Asia	Rest of World
United States	–	0.139	0.156	0.244	0.25	0.008	0.019	0.015	0.079	0.062	0.019
Canada	2.119	–	–	0.004	0.015	–	–	–	0.01	–	–
Mexico	1.642	0.032	–	0.167	0.182	–	–	–	0.006	0.036	0.004
So. America	2.647	0.102	0.04	–	0.239	0.015	–	0.083	0.002	0.106	–
Europe	0.987	0.495	0.01	0.037	–	0.217	–	0.052	0.008	0.097	0.089
FSU	0.282	–	0.002	0.07	5.343	0.02	–	0.365	0.049	0.109	0.2
Middle East	2.505	0.152	0.013	0.164	3.203	0.725	0.135	1.264	4.194	7.213	0.063
No. Africa	0.476	0.14	0.01	0.112	1.924	0.079	–	0.042	0.008	0.117	0.008
West Africa	1.637	0.016	–	0.258	0.542	0.094	0.002	0.551	0.096	0.851	–
East&Southern Africa	–	–	–	–	0.026	–	–	0.116	0.076	0.027	–
Australasia	0.028	–	–	–	0.004	–	–	0.045	0.053	0.093	–
China	0.02	–	–	0.027	0.002	0.002	0.014	–	0.037	0.276	0.006
Japan	0.008	–	–	–	–	–	0.002	0.044	–	0.025	–
Other Asia	0.145	0.004	–	0.004	0.083	0.01	0.495	0.824	0.533	0.284	0.019
Total	**12.496**	**1.08**	**0.231**	**1.087**	**11.813**	**1.17**	**0.667**	**3.401**	**5.151**	**9.296**	**0.40**

Source: Adapted by the authors from BP, *Statistical Review of World Energy 2005*, 18.
Note: U.S. = United States; S&CAm = Central and South America; AusA = Australasia.

The IEA reported that between 1996 and 2004, China's total crude imports increased by more than 440 percent (from 22.8 million tons in 1996 to 122.7 in 2004). According to China's General Administration of Customs, China's imports of Saudi oil increased by 41.3 percent, to reach just above 3 million tons during January and February of 2005, while its imports of Iranian and Omani oil declined.[2]

By the end of 2005, such estimates indicate that China will consume 6.4 mmbpd, second to U.S. consumption of 21 mmbpd. China's consumption by 2020 is projected to triple. The growth of Chinese oil demand is higher than its domestic supply. China's domestic production could reach 3.8 mmbpd in 2020, but its demand is likely to be more than three times as high. In addition, its dependence on Middle Eastern oil has increased from 39.79 percent of its imports in 1994, to 50.99 percent in 2002, and to more than 50 percent in 2004.[3]

Looking at the overall patterns in Asian demand, the EIA estimate for 2005 projects the trends shown in table 4.3. Importantly, the total growth for "other Asia" nearly totals the growth in China. Total Asian demand is estimated to rise from 21.5 mmbpd in 2002 to between 35.6 and 45.50 mmbpd in 2025. As shown, during the same time period India's oil demand is estimated to increase from 2.20 mmbpd to between 4.30 and 5.40 mmbpd, "other Asia's" from 5.6 mmbpd to between 9.80 and 13.4 mmbpd, and South Korea's from 2.20 mmbpd to between 2.60 and 3.40 mmbpd.

EUROPEAN PRESSURE ON DEMAND AND IMPORTS

Tables 4.1 and 4.2 show that Asia is hardly the only region with a thirst for oil. In 2005, the European Union imported 75 percent of its oil and 50 percent of its gas. It is projected that by 2030 these numbers could increase by 90 and 70 percent, respectively, although few absolute increases are projected in European consumption.[4]

If one looks at Western Europe, oil consumption is estimated to rise slowly, from 13.8 mmbpd in 2002 to between 13.7 and 14.4 mmbpd in 2010, between 13.8 and 14.8 mmbpd in 2015, between 13.8 and 15.2 mmbpd in 2020, and between 14.1 and 15.9 mmbpd in 2025. Eastern European growth will also be somewhat faster but much lower. East-

Table 4.3
U.S. EIA Estimate of Trends in Asian Oil Demand, 2002–2025
(million barrels per day)

Country or Region	Total 2002	Total 2025			Increase 2002–2025		
		Low	Reference	High	Low	Reference	High
China	5.20	12.50	14.20	16.10	7.30	9.00	10.90
India	2.20	4.30	4.90	5.40	2.10	2.70	3.20
Other Asia	5.60	9.80	11.60	13.40	4.20	6.00	7.80
Subtotal	13.00	26.60	30.70	34.90	13.60	17.70	21.90
Japan	5.30	5.00	5.30	5.60	-0.30	0.00	0.30
Australia–New Zealand	1.00	1.40	1.50	1.60	0.40	0.50	0.60
South Korea	2.20	2.60	2.90	3.40	0.40	0.70	1.20
Subtotal	8.50	9.00	9.70	10.60	0.50	1.20	2.10
Total	**21.50**	**35.60**	**40.40**	**45.50**	**14.10**	**18.90**	**24.00**

Source: Adapted by the authors from U.S. Energy Information Administration, *International Energy Outlook 2005.*

ern European countries consumed 1.4 mmbpd in 2002. Their consumption is estimated to rise to 1.6 mmbpd in 2010, to between 1.7 and 1.9 mmbpd in 2015, between 1.8 and 2.1 mmbpd in 2020, and between 2.8 and 2.4 mmbpd in 2025.

To put these figures in perspective, total European oil use will rise from 15.2 mmbpd in 2002 to between 15.8 and 18.2 mmbpd in 2025. This is an estimated growth of 0.8 to 3.0 mmbpd. If one looks at the projected growth for the United States over the same period, it will see an increase of 2.1 to 6.2 mmbpd by 2025. Russia is estimated to increase its oil consumption from 2.6 mmbpd in 2002 to between 3.1 and 3.9 mmbpd in 2025, and the rest of FSU from 1.5 mmbpd in 2002 to between 1.8 and 2.3 mmbpd in 2025.

Table 4.4
U.S. EIA Estimate of Trends in Western Oil Demand, 2002–2025
(million barrels per day)

Country or Region	Total 2002	Total 2025			Increase 2002–2025		
		Low	Reference	High	Low	Reference	High
Canada	2.10	2.50	2.60	2.70	0.40	0.50	0.60
United States	2.00	2.80	3.00	2.90	0.80	1.00	0.90
Mexico	23.80	25.90	27.30	30.00	2.10	3.50	6.20
Subtotal	**27.90**	**31.20**	**32.90**	**35.60**	**3.30**	**5.00**	**7.70**
Western Europe	13.80	14.10	14.90	15.90	0.30	1.10	2.10
Eastern Europe	1.40	1.80	2.10	2.40	0.40	0.70	1.00
Subtotal	**15.20**	**15.90**	**17.00**	**18.30**	**0.70**	**1.80**	**3.10**
Russia	2.60	3.10	3.40	3.90	0.50	0.80	1.30
Other former Soviet Union	1.50	1.80	2.00	2.30	0.30	0.50	0.80
Subtotal	**4.10**	**4.90**	**5.40**	**6.20**	**0.80**	**1.30**	**2.10**
Total	**47.20**	**52.00**	**55.30**	**60.10**	**4.80**	**8.10**	**12.90**

Source: Adapted by the authors from U.S. Energy Information Administration, *International Energy Outlook 2005.*

The impact of these trends is shown in table 4.4. Though the growth of total Western demand lags far behind the growth of Asian demand, it still will have a major cumulative impact, and virtually all growth in Western Europe, Eastern Europe, and the United States will have to come from imports.

The EU is looking to expand and strengthen its bilateral relations with the Gulf Cooperation Council (GCC), as the EU energy commissioner, Andris Piebalgs, said, because the GCC is "one of the biggest long-term suppliers of hydrocarbons for the European Union." The EU and the GCC held a conference in Kuwait City in early April 2005 to discuss European–Gulf relations. Some saw the direct negotiations be-

Table 4.5
U.S. EIA Estimate of Trends in Oil Demand in Other Developing Countries, 2002–2025 (million barrels per day)

Region	Total 2002	Total 2025			Increase 2002–2025		
		Low	Reference	High	Low	Reference	High
Africa	2.70	4.40	4.90	5.50	1.70	2.20	2.80
South and Central America	5.20	7.80	9.30	10.40	2.60	4.10	5.20
Middle East	5.70	7.90	9.20	10.50	2.20	3.50	4.80
Total	**13.60**	**20.10**	**23.40**	**26.40**	**6.50**	**9.80**	**12.80**

Source: Adapted by the authors from U.S. Energy Information Administration, *International Energy Outlook 2005.*

tween the EU and the GCC as signaling a crisis, because the IEA traditionally represented oil-consuming nations in such deliberations with oil-producing states. [5]

Oil experts such as John Gault see the EU's move as a response to aggressive Chinese efforts in the Gulf to ensure its access to energy. Gault argues that "competition for access to oil is accelerating and that countries whose governments do not become directly involved risk being left behind." Piebalgs has responded by saying that "it is a more integrated [European energy] market and that means we should have a more integrated policy. . . . That is why the [European] Commission is more active on this issue. But it does not mean that we are taking responsibilities from the IEA."[6]

THE REST OF THE WORLD

While energy analysts focus on Asian growth and growth in the industrialized world, it is important to note that the growth of demand in Africa, the Middle East, and South and Central America also puts pressure on supply and export capacity. These trends are shown in table 4.5. Much of the growth in each of these regions will occur in oil-exporting countries and will reduce the growth of their future export capacity.

Moreover, table 4.5 shows that a very low rate of growth is assumed for Africa. If African economic growth should rise to the level its people need, African demand for oil would be much higher.

GROWING U.S. IMPORT DEPENDENCE AND FAILED ENERGY BILLS AND POLICIES

The United States will be another major factor shaping the growth in world demand for oil and the continuing pressure on supply. This affects energy security as well. Two decades ago, the United States imported oil from economies with stable political systems and few security threats, such as the United Kingdom, Norway, and Alaska. However, for the near future, the United States and the rest of the world have to rely on unstable regions as sources and transition routes for their energy needs.[7]

Figure 4.1 shows recent trends in U.S. import dependence on Gulf states and other oil imported from members of the Organization of the Petroleum Exporting Countries (OPEC). America depends on the Middle East for only part of its imports, and there have been no consistent trends in the percentage of imports the United States gets from OPEC and the Gulf. However, it is all too clear that U.S. oil imports are increasing.

If one looks at OPEC exports as a proportion of U.S. imports, these ranged from 47.8 percent of mmbpd in 1973, to 51.9 percent in 1992, to 39.9 percent in 2002, to 43.6 percent in 2004. If one looks at Gulf exports as a proportion of U.S. imports, they ranged from 13.6 percent of mmbpd in 1973, to 22.5 percent in 1992, to 19.7 percent in 2002, to 19.3 percent in 2004.

The United States has become progressively more dependent on both a growing volume of imports and steadily growing imports from troubled countries and regions. Direct U.S. petroleum imports increased from an annual average of 6.3 mmbpd in 1973, to 7.9 mmbpd in 1992, to 11.3 mmbpd in 2002, to 12.9 mmbpd in 2004. Some 2.5 mmbpd worth of U.S. petroleum imports came directly from the Middle East in 2004.[8] Additionally, the average U.S. petroleum imports from the Persian Gulf alone equaled 2.3 mmbpd in the first six months

Figure 4.1
U.S. Oil Imports and Dependence on OPEC and the Gulf, 1973–2005
(average in thousand barrels per day)

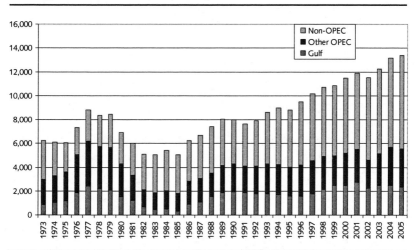

Source: Adapted by the authors from U.S. Energy Information Administration, *Monthly Energy Outlook*, available at: http://www.eia.doe.gov/emeu/mer/overview.html.

of 2005, 2.4 mmbpd in 2004, 2.5 mmbpd in 2003, 2.2 mmbpd in 2002, 2.7 mmbpd in 2001, and 2.4 mmbpd in 2000.[9]

The economic impact of future U.S. increases in import dependence will vary sharply with oil prices. According to March 2005 statistics from the EIA, the oil price "collapse" of late 1997 and 1998 cut U.S. net oil import costs during 1998 by about $20 billion (to $44 billion), compared with the previous two years. Rising oil prices since then have increased U.S. net oil import costs: to $60 billion in 1999, $109 billion in 2000, $94 billion in both 2001 and 2002, and $122 billion in 2003. For the first ten months of 2004, U.S. net oil import costs were running about 31 percent higher than during the same period in 2003. Oil currently accounts for about one-fourth of the total U.S. merchandise trade deficit.

Much of the effort to reduce U.S. dependence on foreign sources of energy has also focused on the instability in the Middle East. As a result, national security and strategic planners in oil-consuming nations have looked to other regions, such as West Africa and the Caspian Sea, to try to find alternative sources of oil supply, in addition to studying the feasibility of alternative energy technologies. So far, such efforts have failed both to find the necessary oil reserves and a mix of nations that are more (or even "as") stable as those of the Gulf and North Africa.

The United States has clear motives for such efforts, and it has reached out into some unexpected areas in such efforts. For example, the U.S. military is investing time and effort in emerging oil regions— planning to spend $100 million to build up the Caspian Guard, a network of police and special operations forces, to protect the new Baku–Tblisi–Ceyhan pipeline, from the Caspian Sea to the Caucasus. The $100 million will also be put toward protecting other energy infrastructures to limit any supply disruption from the Central Asian region. The Caspian Guard also opened a radar-equipped command center in 2003 in Baku, Azerbaijan, to monitor the oil production and export infrastructure. Most of the Caspian Sea oil is exported to Europe, but if supply is disrupted, oil prices will likely rise, and that will have a direct influence on U.S. energy security.[10]

Limited Importance of the Source of U.S. Imports

Under most conditions, the areas and countries the United States and any other country imports from, and the normal day-to-day destination of oil exports, are strategically irrelevant. Oil is a global commodity, which is distributed to meet the needs of a global market based on a bidding process by importers acting in global competition.

With the exception of differences in price because of crude type and transportation costs, buyers and importers compete equally for the global supply of available exports, and the direction and flow of exports change according to marginal price relative to demand. As a result, the percentage of oil that flows from the Middle Eastern and North African region to the United States under normal market conditions has little strategic or economic importance.

If a crisis occurs, or drastic changes take place in prices, and the United States will have to pay the same globally determined price as any other nation, then the source of U.S. imports will change accordingly. Moreover, the United States is required to share all imports with other countries that belong to the Organization for Economic Cooper-

Figure 4.2
Core Petroleum U.S. Import Elasticity Forecast for 2025
(million barrels per day)

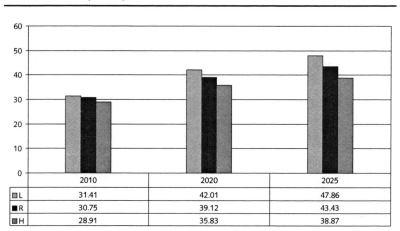

	2010	2020	2025
L	31.41	42.01	47.86
R	30.75	39.12	43.43
H	28.91	35.83	38.87

Source: Adapted by the authors from U.S. Energy Information Administration, *Annual Energy Outlook 2005*, 177.
Note: L = low: $20.99; R = reference: $30.31; H = high: $39.24.

ation and Development during a crisis, under the monitoring of the International Energy Agency.

Estimates of the Potential Growth of U.S. Imports

Looking toward the future, the EIA forecasts in the *Annual Energy Outlook 2005* that total U.S. petroleum imports would reach roughly 21.0 mmbpd by 2025, as table 4.6 shows. This projection is based on somewhat more realistic oil prices (low-price case, $20.99; reference case, $30.31; high-price case, $39.24) than those used in the EIA's 2004 estimates, which have been the basis for the previous discussion of global trends. The EIA forecast for U.S. imports in its 2005 reference case is as follows:

> Total U.S. gross petroleum imports are projected to increase in the reference case from 12.3 million barrels per day in 2003 to 20.2 million in 2025. Crude oil accounts for most of the increase in imports, because distillation capacity at U.S. refineries is expected to be more than 5.5 million barrels per day higher in 2025 than it was in 2003.

Gross imports of refined petroleum, including refined products, unfinished oils, and blending components, are expected to increase by almost 60 percent from 2003 to 2025.

Crude oil imports from the North Sea are projected to decline gradually as North Sea production ebbs. Significant imports of petroleum from Canada and Mexico are expected to continue, with much of the Canadian contribution coming from the development of its enormous oil sands resource base. West Coast refiners are expected to import small volumes of crude oil from the Far East to replace the declining production of Alaskan crude oil. The Persian Gulf share of total gross petroleum imports, 20.4 percent in 2003, is expected to increase to almost 30 percent in 2025; and the OPEC share of total gross imports, which was 42.1 percent in 2003, is expected to be above 60 percent in 2025.

Most of the increase in refined product imports is projected to come from refiners in the Caribbean Basin, North Africa, and the Middle East, where refining capacity is expected to expand significantly. Vigorous growth in demand for lighter petroleum products in developing countries means that U.S. refiners are likely to import smaller volumes of light, low-sulfur crude oils. [11]

If one looks at table 4.6, this estimate indicates that moderate oil prices will lead to major increases in U.S. imports from the Gulf (2.5–6.0 mmbpd), the Americas (3.1–5.0 mmbpd), and "other" including North Africa (2.7–6.2 mmbpd). Figure 4.2 shows, however, that future imports will vary sharply according to price. If prices are low ($20.99/barrel), imports will rise to 47.86 mmbpd in 2025. If prices are moderate ($30.31/barrel), imports will still be 43.43 mmbpd. If prices rise to $39.87 per barrel, however, U.S. imports will be only 38.87 mmbpd, and they would be far lower at $50, $60, $70, or more per barrel. Even the "high-price" case leaves the United States with nearly 60 percent dependence on oil imports in 2025, but the impact of this dependence on world supply is far lower than if oil prices are low or moderate.

In any case, the size of direct U.S. imports of petroleum is only a partial measure of U.S. strategic dependence on imports. The U.S. economy is dependent on energy-intensive imports from Asia and

Table 4.6
U.S. Gross Petroleum Imports by Source, 2000–2025
(million barrels per day)

Year	Gulf	Other OPEC	North America	Europe	Caribbean	Far East	Other	Total
2000	2.49	2.74	3.11	0.96	0.37	0.69	1.10	11.46
2005	2.70	3.25	3.35	1.08	0.41	1.17	0.97	12.93
2010	3.18	3.70	3.53	1.01	0.49	1.28	1.19	14.38
2015	4.28	4.19	4.03	0.93	0.51	1.38	1.12	16.44
2020	5.52	4.77	4.25	0.92	0.50	1.24	0.97	18.17
2025	5.99	6.16	5.01	1.05	0.54	1.18	0.99	20.92

Source: Adapted by the authors from U.S. Energy Information Administration, *Annual Energy Outlook 2005.*

other regions, and what comes around must literally go around. Though the EIA and IEA do not make estimates of indirect imports of oil from the Gulf and other regions in terms of the energy required to produce the finished goods, the United States imports them from countries that are dependent on Middle Eastern exports, and analysts guess that they would add at least 1.0 mmbpd to total U.S. oil imports.

The failure of the U.S. Department of Energy and the EIA to explicitly model indirect imports, and their steady growth, is a long-standing and critical failure in U.S. energy analysis and policy. It seems almost certain that the future increase in such indirect imports will, for example, vastly exceed any benefits in increased domestic energy supply that will result from the energy bill passed by the U.S. Congress in the summer of 2005.

CHINESE IMPORT DEPENDENCE

According to China's state media reports, the country imported 79.9 million tons of oil in first three quarters of 2004, which represented a 40 percent increase from the first eight months of 2003.[12] In 2002, China consumed 5.0 mmbpd. According to EIA 2005 high-price estimates, this number *could* triple by 2025 (12.50 mmbpd for the low-price case, 14.50 mmbpd for the reference case, and 16.1 mmbpd for the high-price case).[13]

According the BP *Statistical Review of World Energy 2005*, Chinese imports totaled 3.40 mmbpd in 2004. China imported 0.15 mmbpd from the United States, 0.038 mmbpd from South and Central America, 0.052 mmbpd from Europe, 0.365 mmbpd from the FSU, 1.264 mmbpd from the Middle East, 0.709 mmbpd from Africa, 0.045 mmbpd from Australasia, 0.044 mmbpd from Japan, 0.824 from other Asia-Pacific, and 0.010 mmbpd from others.[14]

As mentioned above, China's domestic production could reach 3.8 mmbpd in 2020, but its demand is likely to be more than three times as high.[15] During 2004, China imported 40 percent of its oil consumption, despite the fact that it produced 174 million tons of oil during the whole year. Some experts believe that recent high oil prices can provide the right incentives for investment in new technologies to enhance recovery and exploration and increase China's domestic output, thus reducing its reliance on oil imports.[16]

China is aware of its impending total dependence on foreign exporters for oil and petroleum products. In the late 1990s, the Chinese government restructured its oil industry to deal with its high dependence on oil imports. The EIA summarized this reorganization as follows:

China's petroleum industry has undergone major changes over the last decade. In 1998, the Chinese government reorganized most state-owned oil and gas assets into two vertically integrated firms—the China National Petroleum Corporation (CNPC) and the China Petrochemical Corporation (Sinopec). Before the restructuring, CNPC had been engaged mainly in oil and gas exploration and production, while Sinopec had been engaged in refining and distribution. This reorganization created two regionally focused firms—CNPC in the north and west and Sinopec in the south—though CNPC is still tilted toward crude oil production and Sinopec toward refining. The other major state sector firm in China is the China National Offshore Oil Corporation (CNOOC), which handles offshore exploration and production and accounts for more than 10 percent of China's domestic crude oil production. Regulatory oversight of the industry now is the responsibility of the State Energy Administration (SEA), which was created in early 2003.[17]

The major Chinese state oil companies—CNPC, Sinopec, and CNOOC—have aggressively pursued contracts with foreign firms for production and exploration. CNPC has acquired a variety of holdings in Azerbaijan, Canada, Indonesia, Iraq, Iran, Kazakhstan, Venezuela, and Sudan. In November 2004, Sinopec purchased the rights for the development of the Yadavaran oil field in Iran, which is slated to produce 0.300 mmbpd at full capacity.

Sinopec also hopes to import additional petroleum products through its May 2005 acquisition of a 40 percent share in Canada's Northern Lights oil sands project, which is scheduled to be up and running by 2010. CNOOC, the Chinese offshore oil production company, acquired a stake in the small Malacca Strait oil field and made an unsuccessful bid for Unocal, a United States–based firm that opted for a contract with Chevron after pressure from the U.S. Congress not to sell to China.[18]

China has also made notable inroads in the FSU and the far eastern region of Russia. In May 2004, the governments of China and Kazakhstan signed an agreement for a $700 million oil pipeline to run from Atasu in central Kazakhstan to Alashankou in the western Chinese province of Xinjiang, which will have the capacity to supply three Chinese refineries with 0.200 mmbpd of crude oil. China's CNPC also agreed to provide 20 years of development aid to the Kazakh oil firm Aktobemunaigaz after purchasing a 60 percent share in the company in 1997.[19]

The biggest Chinese oil acquisition yet may come from the Canadian oil firm PetroKazakhstan, which has large reserves in Kazakhstan and trades in New York. CNPC has offered $4.18 billion for the company, including $55 cash per share and $76 million toward the creation of an offshoot company led by the current PetroKazakhstan chief executive, Bernard Isautier. Although the proposed plan has not yet been voted upon by the stockholders of the Canadian firm, a binding clause prevents PetroKazakhstan from backing out by threatening a $125 million penalty for accepting a higher offer.[20]

THE OVERALL PATTERNS IN ENERGY IMPORTS

The United States and China are the "drivers" in increasing energy imports in most models—and it should be noted that such models generally do not consider a major recession or depression in such driver economies or on a global basis through 2025. (Trees effectively grow to the sky.) If one looks in detail at the estimates in figure 4.1, however, they are clearly only part of the story, even if one only considers increases in demand.

The previous analysis of the projected total growth in world oil demand between 2002 and 2025 shows that demand growth in other Asia, Europe, the FSU, and the Middle East will also have a major *cumulative* impact, even at sustained high average oil prices. African and Middle Eastern imports could double by 2025. India could emerge as a major new importer, as could other Asian states. Russia could increase domestic consumption sharply in ways that would reduce its exports. Western Europe and Japan are the only major importers not projected to make massive increases in potential demand. Once again, however, the failure to model the high prices or to examine supply by supplier nation in credible terms leaves massive uncertainties.

Notes

[1] BP, *Statistical Review of World Energy 2005*, June 2004, 28.

[2] "Measured Growth," *Foreign Reports Bulletin*, March 22, 2005.

[3] Jin Liangziang, "Energy First: China and the Middle East," *Middle East Quarterly*, Spring 2005, available at http://www.meforum.org/article/694.

[4] Thomas Catan, "Fears of Energy Squeeze Prompt Talks," *Financial Times*, April 4, 2005.

[5] Ibid.

[6] Ibid.

[7] John J. Fialka, "Search for Crude Comes with New Dangers," *Wall Street Journal*, April 11, 2005.

[8] BP, *Statistical Review of World Energy 2005*, June 2003, 17.

[9] U.S. Energy Information Administration (EIA), "Petroleum Imports from Qatar, Saudi Arabia, U.A.E. and Total Persian Gulf," *Monthly Energy Review*, August 2005, available at http://www.eia.doe.gov/emeu/mer/pdf/pages/sec3_9.pdf.

[10] Fialka, "Search for Crude."

[11] EIA, *Annual Energy Outlook 2005*, available at http://www.eia.doe.gov/oiaf/aeo/economic.html.

[12] "China Reports Soaring Oil Imports," BBC News, available at http://news.bbc.co.uk/1/hi/business/3654060.stm.

[13] EIA, *International Energy Outlook 2005*, July 2005.

[14] BP, *Statistical Review of World Energy 2005*, June 2005, 18.

[15] Jin, "Energy First."

[16] "China to Control Its Reliance on Oil Imports," *Xinhua*, April 23, 2005, available at http://www2.chinadaily.com.cn/english/doc/2005-04/23/content_436862.htm#.

[17] EIA, Country Analysis Brief, "China," available at http://www.eia.doe.gov/emeu/cabs/china.html.

[18] Ibid.

[19] Ibid.

[20] "Economic Brief: China's Energy Acquisitions," *Power and Interest News Report*, September 2, 2005, available at http://www.pinr.com/report.php?ac=view_report&report_id=359&language_id=1.

CHAPTER FIVE

REGIONAL STRATEGIC AND PRODUCTION RISKS

The global trends in supply have major uncertainties of their own, but it is questionable that oil-producing and oil-exporting countries can actually meet the current estimates of future demand in everything but the high-price case. Figures 5.1 and 5.2 show recent trends in estimates of oil reserves and oil production by region. The geopolitical risks in every region can take many forms. The security of oil facilities is most obvious, but the stability of sovereign governments is also central to preventing supply disruptions and ensuring the safety of trade routes.

In 2005, the International Energy Agency (IEA) summarized its apprehensions about energy security as follows:

> Serious concerns about energy security emerge from the market trends. . . . The world's vulnerability to supply disruptions will increase as international trade expands. Climate destabilizing carbon-dioxide emissions will continue to rise, calling into question the sustainability of the current energy system. Huge amounts of new energy infrastructure will need to be financed. And many of the world's poorest people will still be deprived of modern energy services. These challenges call for urgent and decisive action by governments around the world. [1]

Moreover, given the interdependence of the global market, perceptions of instability are as important as realities. To reassure markets, producers have to build confidence not only in their capability to prevent attacks but also in their ability to contain the damage of unex-

Figure 5.1
World Proven Oil Reserves Trends, 1984–2004 (billion barrels)

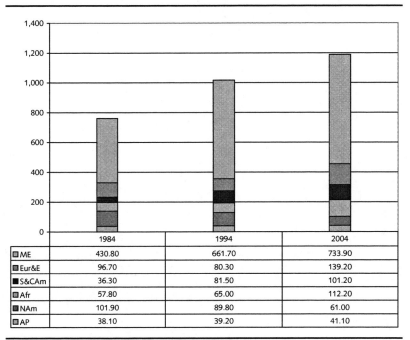

	1984	1994	2004
ME	430.80	661.70	733.90
Eur&E	96.70	80.30	139.20
S&CAm	36.30	81.50	101.20
Afr	57.80	65.00	112.20
NAm	101.90	89.80	61.00
AP	38.10	39.20	41.10

Source: Adapted by the authors from BP, *Statistical Review of World Energy 2005.*
Note: ME = Middle East; Eur&E = Europe and Eurasia; S&CAm = South and Central
America; Afr = Africa; NAm = North America; AP = Asia Pacific.

pected violence by building redundancy into production and export
systems.

Since the start of terrorist attacks in Saudi Arabia in May 2003, the
Kingdom has increased the security and redundancy of its oil infrastructure, including its oil reservoirs, export terminals, and refineries
on the Red Sea and the Gulf. The attempted attacks in the Saudi cities
of Yanbu and Al-Khubar in the summer of 2004 sent ripples throughout the global energy market. The redundancy of the Saudi export and
production systems, along with the swiftness of the Saudi forces in
suppressing the attacks, reassured the global market.[2]

Attempts against Saudi oil, however, continue to worry the global
energy market and the Saudi leadership. Following a siege and a raid
by the Saudi security forces against extremists in Dammam, these forc-

Figure 5.2
World Oil Production Trends, 1984–2004 (million barrels per day)

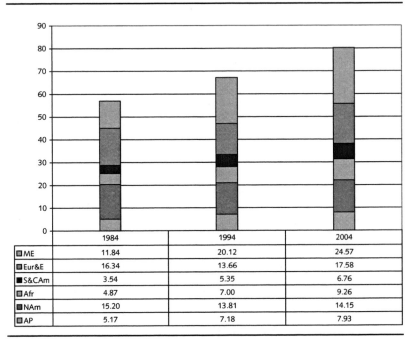

	1984	1994	2004
ME	11.84	20.12	24.57
Eur&E	16.34	13.66	17.58
S&CAm	3.54	5.35	6.76
Afr	4.87	7.00	9.26
NAm	15.20	13.81	14.15
AP	5.17	7.18	7.93

Source: Adapted by the authors from BP, *Statistical Review of World Energy 2005*.
Note: ME = Middle East; Eur&E =Europe and Eurasia; S&CAm = South and Central
America; Afr = Africa; NAm = North America; AP = Asia Pacific.

es discovered more than 60 hand grenades and pipe bombs, pistols, machine guns, rocket-propelled grenades, two barrels full of explosives, and video equipment. The Saudi minister of the interior, Prince Nayef al-Saud, was quoted as saying that an Al Qaeda cell had planned to attack Saudi oil and gas infrastructure, but Prince Nayef added, "There isn't a place that they could reach that they didn't think about," and he insisted that Al Qaeda's ultimate goal has been to cripple the global economy.[3]

These problems are scarcely unique to Saudi Arabia. Other exporters in the Middle East, Africa, and Latin America already have more serious internal security problems. According to Ian McCredie, the head of Shell's Global Security Services, 14 oil-producing regions have local security forces that are "largely ineffective." Oil companies have experienced kidnappings by rebel and guerrilla groups in Africa and Latin America, threats of terrorist attacks in the Middle East, danger of piracy in the Malacca Straits for oil tankers, and expropriation and "industrial espionage" in Russia.[4]

Since the start of the Iraq War in March 2003, Iraq's oil infrastructure has suffered many attacks by insurgents against its pipelines and refineries. According to the Institute for the Analysis of Global Security, there have been more than 200 attacks against Iraqi gas and oil installations since June 2003.[5] There has been little evidence, however, that insurgents have attempted to attack or successfully attacked large oil fields in the north and the south.

Oil fields are large-area targets with many redundant facilities. Though fires can be set in many areas of a working field, including at oil wells, fires do not produce critical or lasting damage. Unless wells are attacked with explosives deep enough in the wellhead to result in permanent damage to the well, most facilities can be rapidly repaired.

There are, however, larger items of equipment and central facilities, which if damaged would do far more to interrupt production, and many of which would require months of manufacturing time to replace. Such facilities include central pumping facilities, gas-oil separators, related power plants, water injection facilities, and desalination plants. Vulnerability also increases sharply if key targets in a field are attacked as a system rather than as individual elements, and if expert assistance is available to saboteurs or attackers.

It is impossible to eliminate the threat against energy infrastructure from conventional military attacks, asymmetric warfare by extremists, or proliferation. However, the recent security efforts by the Saudi government—for example, the overlapping and redundant layers of defense around key installations, and the extensive disaster planning and drills that have taken place—have significantly lessened the probability of any major attacks being carried out successfully.

Short of a spectacular strike on the scale of September 11, 2001, or some form of systematic sabotage of key energy industries, most foreseeable assaults are likely to be quickly confined and any resulting damage is likely to be repaired relatively quickly. However, energy security will be a continuing problem, particularly if global energy demand does actually rise by more than 50 percent by 2025. The security of energy exports will play a steadily more vital role in the world's economy.

The Middle East makes a good case in point. In the past two decades, the Middle East and Africa have experienced the largest increase in oil production of any region. As is shown in figure 5.2, in 1983, Africa produced 4.9 million barrels per day (mmbpd) and the Middle East produced 11.8 mmbpd; but by 2004, these numbers reached 9.3 and 24.6 mmbpd, respectively. Production levels of other regions remained at approximately the same level as in the 1980s.

Most of the growth in reserves in the past two decades has come from the Middle East, and from the Gulf. In 1983, the Middle East's "proven" reserves were 396.9 billion barrels of oil; in 2004, that number had nearly doubled to 733.9 billion. Other regions, however, also saw substantial growth in their reserves. Latin America's proven oil reserves increased from 33.7 billion barrels in 1983 to 101.20 billion barrels in 2004. Though only North America has had its proven oil reserves decline during the same period, the Asia-Pacific region has seen little growth in its proven reserves.

Although a nation like Iran can pose a conventional and asymmetric military threat to oil facilities in the Gulf, the more dangerous threat is that of asymmetric attacks by extremist groups on oil facilities in the Gulf, where 65 percent of the world's proven reserves exist. There is no attack-proof security system. It may take only one attack on Ghawar or a tanker in the Strait of Hormuz to throw the global oil market into a spiral.

In addition to current asymmetric threats posed by rogue states and terrorist organizations, there is a growing risk that such states and groups may acquire the capability to use weapons of mass destruction (WMD) to blackmail oil-producing states for economic or political reasons. Recent success in stopping the A. Q. Khan network does not mean the end of the WMD black market. Russian loose nuclear devices and disenfranchised former Soviet Union (FSU) scientists continue to be a source of expertise for extremists and rogue states that are trying to acquire the technology.

Regional stability is multilayered. Social and political stability is as important as effective security. Labor strikes in Venezuela, hurricanes in the Gulf of Mexico, the Iraq War, and the ongoing disruptions of Angolan and Nigerian oil compounded by surging oil demand are examples of what could hike the price to $70 a barrel.

Supply and demand pressures play a major role in determining the price of oil, but they cannot explain the energy market. Regional geopolitical and production challenges exert pressure on oil prices, but it is hard to quantify these risks. The following sections attempt to outline midterm and long-term strategic challenges for oil-producing regions as well as production developments and risks associated with the nature of resources, technological developments, and management issues, including field maintenance and the cost of production.

THE MIDDLE EAST

The data given in previous chapters have shown that the Middle East is estimated to have 62 percent of the world's conventional oil reserves in 2005 (733.90 billion barrels) and currently generates 23 percent of total world production (24.57 mmbpd). The Middle East still has roughly 53 percent of the world's reserves, even if Canadian tar sands are included (some estimate that the tar sands contain 175 billion barrels of oil). The Middle East also has 40.6 percent (2,570.8 trillion cubic feet, or tcf) of the world's total gas reserves (6,337.4 tcf).

Figures 5.1 and 5.2 show that the Middle East has dominated world production and reserves, and that it has seen the largest historical growth in both. In figure 5.3, the Middle East has an estimated 672.6 billion barrels of "known" reserves, 204.8 billion barrels of "undiscovered" reserves, and 728.7 billion barrels of "proven" reserves. The definition of each type of reserve may be summarized as follows:

- *Proven reserves:* Quantities of crude oil that geological data and engineering information indicate with reasonable certainty can be recovered in the future.

- *Known reserves:* Discovered crude oil accumulations that are considered economically viable to produce.

- *Undiscovered reserves:* Quantities of crude oil that geological data and engineering information indicate exist outside known oil fields.

Figure 5.3
Middle East Proven, Known, Undiscovered Oil Reserves
(billion barrels)

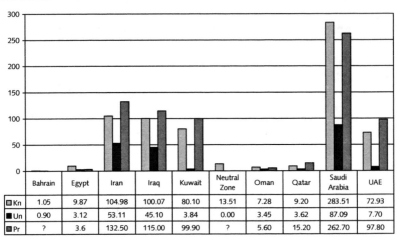

	Bahrain	Egypt	Iran	Iraq	Kuwait	Neutral Zone	Oman	Qatar	Saudi Arabia	UAE
Kn	1.05	9.87	104.98	100.07	80.10	13.51	7.28	9.20	283.51	72.93
Un	0.90	3.12	53.11	45.10	3.84	0.00	3.45	3.62	87.09	7.70
Pr	?	3.6	132.50	115.00	99.90	?	5.60	15.20	262.70	97.80

Source: Adapted by the authors from BP, *Statistical Review of World Energy 2005*, and the *U.S. Geological Survey 2000*.
Note: Kn = known; Un = undiscovered; Pr = proven.

Some 40 percent of all world oil exports, and roughly one-quarter of world supply, now pass daily through the Strait of Hormuz. Projections by both the U.S. Energy Information Agency (EIA) and the IEA indicate that this total will increase to about 60 percent between 2025 and 2030 at low oil prices. An examination of the EIA estimates further indicates that this figure will still be about 50 percent in the high-price case.[6]

Current IEA projections indicate that Middle Eastern exports could total some 46 mmbpd by 2030, and represent more that two-thirds of the world's total exports—although it must be stressed that such projections are based on relatively low prices. This means that the daily traffic in oil tankers will increase from 15 mmbpd and 44 percent of global interregional trade in 2002 to 43 mmbpd and 66 percent of global interregional trade in 2030.

It also means that the daily traffic in liquefied natural gas (LNG) carriers will increase from 28 billion cubic meters and 18 percent of global interregional trade in 2002 to 230 carriers and 34 percent of global interregional trade in 2030.[7] The IEA does, however, estimate that these increases would be some 11 percent lower if oil prices remained consistently high in constant dollars.

A combination of massive reserves and comparatively low incremental production costs seems likely to ensure that the region will continue to dominate increases in the world's oil production capacity regardless of probable variations in oil prices—at least through 2015 and quite possibly through 2025. Much does, however, depend on the long-term trend in world oil prices.

As has been discussed earlier, the IEA projected that world oil demand will increase by 60 percent between 2004 and 2030, and the EIA forecasts that total world oil demand will increase by roughly 40 percent during the same period. Most analysts do believe that world dependence on Middle Eastern oil will increase and that the members of the Organization of the Petroleum Exporting Countries (OPEC) in the Middle East will meet most of the increase in demand. In the real world, however, many factors drive the behavior of countries in the Middle East in determining their production capacity.

Energy investment and development are affected by both security issues and economic forces. It is far too soon to make long-term predictions about what Middle Eastern and North African states will do in response to economic forces if prices and revenues remain high. It is clear from EIA country surveys, however, that high prices, high demand, and high revenues have prompted most Middle Eastern countries to either increase production capacity or develop new plans to do so. The exceptions are those counties with major political or internal security problems.

Figure 5.4 shows the EIA production capacity forecast for selected countries in the Middle East. In 2025, for the reference case, the Middle East will have a production capacity of 42.6.6 mmbpd, compared with 30.6 mmbpd for the high-price case, which represents a 91 percent or 34 percent increase from its production capacity in 2002, respectively. As mentioned above, these projections are based on oil prices that are almost certainly unrealistically low (the high-price case used $48/barrel, while the reference case used $35/barrel).

Figure 5.4
U.S. EIA Estimates of Middle East Oil Production Capacity
(million barrels per day)

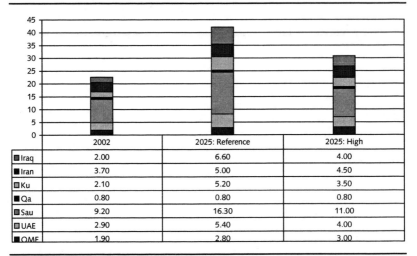

	2002	2025: Reference	2025: High
▨ Iraq	2.00	6.60	4.00
▪ Iran	3.70	5.00	4.50
▨ Ku	2.10	5.20	3.50
▪ Qa	0.80	0.80	0.80
▨ Sau	9.20	16.30	11.00
▨ UAE	2.90	5.40	4.00
▪ OME	1.90	2.80	3.00

Source: Adapted by the authors from U.S. Energy Information Administration,
International Energy Outlook 2005.
Note: Ku = Kuwait; Qa = Qatar; Sau = Saudi Arabia; UAE = United Arab Emirates;
OME = Other Middle East.

According to the EIA *Monthly Energy Review,* the OPEC Gulf countries produced 22.65 mmbpd in 2002. The EIA, however, projects that the Gulf will produce 39.3 mmbpd in 2025 for its reference-case forecast, 27.8 mmbpd for its high-price forecast, and 50.0 mmbpd for its low-price forecast. Similarly, the IEA projected that production from the Gulf will double by 2030, but this was based on relatively low oil prices. The IEA *World Energy Outlook 2004* concluded, "A disruption in supply at any of these points could have a severe impact on oil markets. Maintaining the security of international sea-lanes and pipelines will take on added urgency."[8]

National Developments

It is important to note that the growth of the real-world export capacity of the Middle East region will probably fall short. Most projections of demand for Middle Eastern oil exports will be supply-limited, regardless of future oil prices. The demand-driven modeling of the IEA and the EIA has a fantasy-like character in assuming purely market-driven increases in Middle Eastern country export capacity regardless of real world political, economic, and oil field development constraints. It also seems to be based on unrealistically low development and future export costs.

At the same time, the strategic importance of Middle Eastern oil exporters will not alter significantly if the Middle East cannot expand exports and production capacity to the projected level. If anything, their importance increases in economic and strategic impact if global supply remains under constant stress because of high levels of demand. Let us briefly look at the situation of each exporting country.

Bahrain: Bahrain has proven oil reserves of only 125 million barrels, and its production levels have been steadily declining since the 1970s. In addition, it produces only refined petroleum products, so it must import crude oil to meet its domestic demand. However, the Bahrain Petroleum Company (Bapco) recently finished a $900 million project that increased production capacity, allowing Bahrain to produce a wider range of petroleum products.

Bahrain has long-standing political tensions between its Sunni elite and Shiite majority, which could explode into open civil conflict, lead to Iranian covert or overt intervention, and/or bring down its royal family. Sectarian tensions are compounded by structural economic problems resulting from the depletion of oil reserves, the growing population, and an overdependence on foreign labor.

Iraq: Although the U.S. and Iraqi governments have given a high priority to restoring Iraqi oil production and exports, an increasingly violent and destabilizing low-intensity conflict in the reconstruction period has caused oil and gas production to fall. In the first six months of 2005, oil production averaged only 1.9 mmbpd, versus 2.6 mmbpd before the invasion of Iraq.[9]

Funds that have been appropriated by the United States to the Iraqi oil sector have been diverted to security efforts, as the violence has increased and the need for basic infrastructure outside the oil sector has proved to be more expensive than originally estimated.[10] More damage has been inflicted on vital infrastructure by looting than fighting during the conflict. The Institute for the Analysis of Global Security estimates that there were 267 attacks on Iraqi oil infrastructure and personnel between June 2003 and September 2005. [11]

Although security issues have constantly affected the development of Iraq's northern fields, its southern fields have remained unscathed in this regard. However, the lack of adequate U.S. investment in repairs to these fields has contributed to the low production levels, which have actually declined in the past year and are much lower than target levels. Some estimate that if repairs were completed on schedule, Iraq would currently be producing an additional 0.5 mmbpd, which translates into an additional $8 billion in annual revenue. [12]

There are no current plans from major oil companies to develop the Iraqi oil industry and fix these problems in the near future, which suggests that it will be several years at least before Iraq can achieve the 5.5 mmbpd production that experts predicted could be made possible by its extensive reserves. Issam al-Chalabi, the Iraqi oil minister in the 1980s, told a London conference, "There is no plan to develop the Iraqi oil industry." In addition, he notes that articles 109 and 112 of the newly drafted Iraqi Constitution are contradictory in terms of who is in charge of the oil industry—the federal authority or the separate provinces. Thamir Abbas Ghadbhan, a current leader of the Iraqi oil industry, notes that 24 million liters of oil are needed each day, compared with only 10 million liters of current production, requiring Iraq to import additional oil to meet its domestic demand. [13]

Another aspect of the stagnation in Iraq's oil sector is its aging equipment and technology. Iraq's oil equipment has not been upgraded since the late 1980s due to the sanctions during Saddam Hussein's regime. The lack of an upgrade of the vital oil infrastructure is compounded the fact that Iraq still uses oil extraction practices that are damaging to the reservoirs, such as residual fuel reinjection in the oil wells of Kirkuk and the ongoing practice of excessive water injection in some of the northern oil fields. [14]

Three key projects in Iraqi oil reconstruction are not going as planned, which will likely add to the total price of restoring the Iraqi economy and limit overall economic growth and recovery. In addition, much of the tension among the Sunnis, Shiites, and Kurds during the drafting of the Iraqi Constitution was largely over how oil and gas revenues will be divided. Unless these issues can be resolved in ways that all of Iraq's factions can accept, political struggle over oil revenues and development is likely to further postpone Iraq's national development and increase the instability of the region, as well as retard the growth of Iraq's economy, cripple the political structure, and lower social welfare. It is expected that Iraq's economic and social problems will continue well beyond 2010, even under the best of circumstances.

More broadly, Iraq's growing sectarian and ethnic tensions, ongoing insurgency, and risk of an escalating civil war make it at least a moderate midterm risk to both maintain current export levels and provide a stable climate for major future investment and development.

Iran: Although Iran remains the Gulf's second-largest oil producer and holds the world's fourth-largest pool of proven oil reserves (132.50 billion barrels of oil), its production has dropped by more than a third from its peak levels before the fall of the shah to 2005 levels of 4.1 mmbpd.[15] The EIA projects that Iran's production capacity in 2025 will still be either 4.5 or 5.0 mmbpd, for high-price and reference cases, respectively.

Iran does contain the world's second largest gas reserves, totaling an estimated 940 tcf. Dramatic recent increases in energy prices and net oil exports have the potential to significantly improve the country's economy, but it retains a massive budget deficit that is exacerbated by the refusal of the Majlis to raise consumer prices. In January 2005, the Majlis froze domestic prices for oil and other fuels at 2003 levels, maintaining prices lower than 40 cents per gallon of gasoline.[16]

Both 2004's election of the Majlis and 2005's presidential election have strengthened the hand of Iran's hard-liners and those who oppose a major foreign role in Iran's oil and gas development. Iran has also shown only limited realism in trying to develop oil and gas projects and offer incentives for foreign investment. These internal problems have interacted with U.S. sanctions, which have had at least a limited impact.

Tehran cannot achieve its ambitious production goals without tens of billions of dollars in investment; however, its laws prohibit the

granting of petroleum rights to any private company on a concession-
ary basis or for a direct equity stake. In addition, the situation of Iran's
nuclear program remains uncertain. If the case is referred to the UN
Security Council and sanctions are imposed, it may make it harder for
Iran to attract any meaningful foreign investment to its energy sector.

Kuwait: Kuwait contains an estimated 99.9 billion barrels of proven
oil reserves, or approximately 8.3 percent of the world total. Its gas reserves are among the world's top 20 (1.57 trillion cubic meters, or 0.9
percent of the world's reserves). Its oil sector showed promise at the
official end of combat for the Iraq War, due to Kuwaiti involvement in
Iraqi development contracts and the possibility of collaboration on
energy projects, but security issues have dampened prior optimism. In
addition, two border incidents in July 2005 have forced a renewed dispute over land and the Ratqa-Rumaila oil fields into the public are-
na.[17]

Kuwait's oil wealth should be enough to support the needs of its
population with only limited economic reform and diversification,
and the government already maintains a "Future Generations Fund,"
to which it deposits 10 percent of all oil revenues, to be tapped into
when the oil supply runs out. The government has also proposed
Project Kuwait, a $7-billion, 25-year plan to increase the nation's oil
production with help from international firms; however, final approv-
al must come from the Kuwaiti Parliament, whose nationalist and Islamist members have stood firm in their opposition to foreign
involvement in the country's energy sector.[18]

Kuwait has been attempting to expand its state-owned investments
in petrochemicals, export facilities, and Middle Eastern and North African regional pipeline networks. There is broad agreement in the
world oil industry, however, that the result has been to provide inade-
quate investment in development and new technology, and possibly to
reduce Kuwait's ultimate recovery from the fields it is currently exploiting.

Kuwait has moderate internal stability. The regime has weak top
leadership, and the strength of Islamist movements is growing, fueled
in part by the backlash to the Iraq War.

Kuwait does not yet seem to face significant internal security threats. It does, however, seem to face a "security dilemma"; it enjoys a U.S. security blanket but has to balance this with the social forces that are increasingly of an Islamist nature. Furthermore, experts note that younger generations of Kuwaitis did not have to suffer Saddam Hussein's invasion of their country and thus do not appreciate the role the United States played in liberating their country.

A high birthrate has given Kuwait a young population, and the young people are increasingly anti-American because of both the war in Iraq and U.S. support for Israel. It has been reported that Kuwaiti nationals are among the insurgents in Iraq. Furthermore, radicals in Kuwait have attacked U.S. convoys on their way to Iraq, and there were investigations of a possible plot to assassinate the interim Iraqi prime minister, Iyad Allawi, who was visiting Kuwait on the fourteenth anniversary of the Iraqi invasion.[19]

Oman: Oman does not have large oil resources. Its oil fields are generally smaller, more widely scattered, less productive, and more costly to produce than in other Gulf countries, due to their extensive use of enhanced oil recovery (EOR) techniques to maximize production. Figure 5.3 shows that Oman has 7.28 billion barrels of known reserves, 3.45 billion barrels of undiscovered reserves, and 5.60 billion barrels of proven reserves.

Oman has made a substantial effort to diversify its economy by exploiting other available natural resources, by developing a domestic manufacturing base, and through "Omanization," a program intended to employ more Omani citizens in the private sector. Currently, only 10 percent of workers in private firms are Omani nationals. Despite these efforts to diversify its economy, Oman continues to be heavily dependent on oil revenues. For example, in 2004, oil revenues accounted for 75 percent of its export earnings and roughly 40 percent of its gross domestic product.[20]

Oman has been successful in attracting foreign investment to its energy sector as part of its continuing effort to diversify its economy and develop domestic value-added industries. It is planning to seek additional foreign investment in petrochemical production, and it is involved with the promising Dolphin Project. Oman began supplying gas to Dolpin Energy Limited in late 2003, although plans call for the pipeline flow to eventually reverse, supplying Oman with gas from Qatar to be used in petrochemical and fertilizer plants. However, Oman has been left with more bureaucratic restrictions, its labor productivity remains low, and political reforms have been minimal.

Oman is having limited problems with Islamist extremists. In addition, the political succession process in Oman is uncertain. There are no obvious successors to Sultan Qaboos, and it remains unclear if the Omani political system has evolved enough to deal with a lack of leadership at the top.

Qatar: Qatar is primarily a gas power, but figure 5.3 shows that it has 9.20 billion barrels of known oil reserves, 3.62 billion barrels of undiscovered reserves, and 15.20 billion barrels of proven reserves. Due to its extensive oil revenues coupled with a small population, Qatar has 80 percent of the wealth per capita of the European average. The Qatari economy grew at the high rate of 7.0 percent in 2004, with a 6.7 percent growth level predicted for 2005.

Qatar has a high foreign debt ($17 billion in 2004) and an increasing rate of inflation, which is projected to reach 4.1 percent in 2005, largely due to significant investments in infrastructure to increase production capacity for oil and gas. Nevertheless, the country has maintained a net revenue surplus in recent years, allowing government allocations for infrastructure and development to total 22 percent of its overall budget for 2004–2005. All the additional capacity will go toward exports, because oil makes up less than 15 percent of domestic energy consumption, a number that is already low due to the small population.[21]

A sharp rise in oil and gas export revenues has allowed Qatar to allocate much more money toward the development of its oil fields, and the pace and scope of its projects has significantly improved. It is also pressing ahead with several high-priority gas projects, including the construction of new liquefaction facilities, the Dolphin Project, and an expansion of exports to the Asian market, adding India to its client list of the world's two largest LNG importers, Japan and South Korea.[22]

Qatar had several clashes with Saudi Arabia before the two countries finally agreed on a border settlement, and Qatar accused several of its southern Gulf neighbors of supporting a coup attempt by the present emir's deposed father. Qatari–Saudi relations, however, continue to be tenuous at best, due to Qatar's support of the Al Jazeera network and its desire to sign a free trade agreement with the United States.

In addition, some Saudis believe that Qatar's foreign minister, Sheikh Hamad bin Jassim al-Thani, has made comments that may undermine the Saudi Peace Initiative, which promised normalization of Arab–Israeli relations if Israel withdrew to the 1967 border. On September 15, 2005, the foreign minister suggested that it is possible for Qatar to establish full diplomatic relations with Israel even before a full withdrawal.[23]

Qatar has so far been able to maintain good relations with Iran in developing the giant gas field the two countries share in the Gulf. Though Iran is the primary potential threat, there have never been serious tensions between the two countries. The future is, however, uncertain.

Saudi Arabia: Saudi Arabia is the world's preeminent oil power. Figure 5.3 shows that it has 283.51 billion barrels of known oil reserves, 87.09 billion barrels of undiscovered reserves, and 262.70 billion barrels of proven reserves. Saudi Aramco recently announced that it plans to reach production capacity levels of 12.05 mmbpd by 2009, followed by an additional increase to 15.0 mmbpd "if the market situation justifies it."[24] The EIA forecasts that in 2025, Saudi production capacity will reach 16.30 mmbpd in its reference-case forecast and 11.0 mmbpd in its high-price forecast.

The Kingdom's current capacity is estimated to be between 10.5 and 11.0 mmbpd, which includes the increase from Abu Safah and Qatif. An estimated 2.3 to 2.4 mmbpd of new capacity will come onstream between 2005 and 2009, but an estimated 0.8 mmbpd of that will go into replenishing the natural decline curve. The end result is a net addition of roughly 1.6 mmbpd to the current sustainable capacity of 11.0 mmbpd. This addition increases the sustainable capacity to 12.5 mmbpd of by 2009. According to Aramco's senior vice president for exploration and production, Abdullah Al-Saif, the capacity expansion program has been put on a fast track, and the fields may come on-stream before 2009.[25]

The investment cost for Saudi Arabia's plan for future capacity expansion is estimated to be about $15 billion. It was also reported that, during the same period, the Kingdom's total investment in the petroleum sector was estimated to total $50 billion.[26] Experts believe that the latter number represents Saudi Arabia's total energy investment, while the $15 billion represents the cost of the projects outlined above.

Whatever the debates over Saudi capacity may be today, these projects and dates now provide clear benchmarks for measuring Saudi capacity and credibility. Success will greatly enhance all aspects of Saudi credibility. Failure will be an important strategic warning.

Saudi Aramco has a proven record of success in consistent oil exploration and construction. There is a need, however, to make massive further increases in gas exploration and development, which comes at the same time that the Kingdom must fund oil development, restructure the rest of its economy, and meet rapidly growing civil demands from its rising population.[27]

There have been serious internal debates over privatization and opening the energy industry to foreign investment. Additionally, there is a heightened security risk since Al Qaeda's terrorist attacks in May 2003, which has required the Saudi government to spend additional funds to protect oil installations. Attacks on the Abqaiq oil-processing facilities have the potential to cut the current oil output of 9.6 mmbpd by 4.0 mmbpd, a scenario that could sustain itself for two months or more.[28]

Although details of the Saudi security budget are classified, it was estimated to total more than $8.0 billion in 2004. Between 2002 and 2004, the Saudi government allocated approximately $1.2 billion to increase security at all its energy facilities. At any one time, it is estimated that there are between 25,000 and 30,000 troops protecting the Kingdom's oil infrastructure. "For years, Saudi Arabia has recognized the importance of protecting its vital facilities, long before the recent terrorist actions. So we've always maintained a high level of security," says Abdullatif Othman, the executive director of Saudi Aramco affairs.[29]

As for long-term Saudi plans, the oil minister, Ali Al-Naimi, in an address to the Royal Institute of International Affairs in London in November 2004, talked about the Kingdom's quest to build up its production capacity to deal with recent developments in the international oil market:[30]

We have also recently developed plans to increase gradually Saudi Arabia's sustainable production capacity to 12.5 million barrels per day (bpd). These plans call for a substantial amount of work in both new and old oil fields over the next few years. Fields and reservoirs for the expansion program have already been identified. . . .

The decision to invest in added production capacity on this scale reflects our belief that demand for Saudi oil will continue to increase through the coming years. For the longer term, scenarios to raise the capacity to 15 million bpd have also been studied and can be set in motion if the global demand requires it. . . .

[The Kingdom believes] a reasonable spare capacity of no less than 1.5 million bpd. As in the past, the spare capacity helps assure the continuity of stable oil markets by making more oil available in times of supply dislocations or any unusual surge in demand. . . .

[Aramco] was able to advance its production capacity on a sustainable basis from 7.0 million to 10.0 million bpd during the first half of the 1990s, a permanent increase of some 3.0 million bpd, all the while finding new reserves to replace its production.

It is not clear exactly whether, how, and how long Saudi Arabia could reach and sustain production levels of 12.5 or 15.0 mmbpd, although this may well be possible.

Saudi midterm plans are much clearer. Most of its present spare capacity comes from Safaniyah. The estimates for the Safaniyah capacity range from 1.2 to 1.5 mmbpd, and they come from two onshore wet-crude handling facilities with two trains of 0.60 mmbpd. The Saudi Aramco Crude Expansion Program in the 1980s "recompleted" 60 oil wells that were in the shutoff zones to access lower reservoirs that have been mixed with water. The oil from Safaniyah does not need to be stabilized before shipment because it lacks hydrogen sulfide, but Safaniyah lacks high conversion refining capacity.[31]

Table 5.1
Increase in Saudi Production Capacity by Field, 2005–2009

Oil Field	Grade	Estimated Cost (billions of dollars)	New Capacity (millions of barrels per day)	Espected Date
Abu Safah and Qatif	Arab light and extra light	4.0	0.50–0.55	2004/2005
Haradh	Arab light	1.0	0.30	2006
Khursaniyah	Arab light and extra light	4.0	0.50	2007
Shaybah	Arab extra light	1.5	0.40–0.50	2008
Khoreis	Arab extra light	6.0	1.0–1.2	2009
Total		**16.5**	**2.70–3.05**	**2004–2009**

Source: Adapted by the authors from the Saudi National Security Assessment Project, 2005.

In 2004, the Kingdom developed two oil fields, Qatif and Abu Safah. These fields have an onstream production capability of 0.80 mmbpd. These projects increased Saudi Arabia's production capacity from 10.5 to 11.0 mmbpd. In 2004, Al-Naimi said that Saudi Aramco "regularly develops and brings onstream major new crude oil increments such as the Arabian Super Light crude from fields south of Riyadh and the massive Shaybah field in the Empty Quarter with its 0.50 mmbpd production increment."[32]

In March 2005, Aramco awarded five projects worth $8 billion to foreign firms. The projects are expected to be finished in 2007 and will boost the Kingdom's capacity. The goal is produce 0.50 mmbpd from Kharsaniya and 0.31 mmbpd in LNG from Hawiya.[33]

Table 5.1 summarizes the expected future increases in the Kingdom's production capacity resulting from new projects. As shown, between 2004 and 2009, Saudi production capacity is estimated to increase by 2.7 to 3.05 mmbpd. The new oil will be of light or extra-light grade. Most of the increase will come from Khoreis' approximately 1.0 mmbpd. It is notable that the Kingdom announced in 2005 that it had the objective of reaching 12.50 mmbpd in sustained oil production capacity. Its current capacity is estimated to be between 10.8 and 11.0 mmbpd, which includes the increase from Abu Safah and Qatif.

United Arab Emirates: Figure 5.3 shows that the United Arab Emirates (UAE) has 72.93 billion barrels of known oil reserves, 7.70 billion barrels of undiscovered reserves, and 97.80 billion barrels of proven reserves. The UAE's 97.8 billion barrels of proven reserves account for almost 8 percent of the world total.[34] It is currently in the process of expanding production capacity in several of its fields (its immediate goal being to raise overall production capacity to 3.5 mmbpd in one year), but it needs foreign investment in these expansion projects—not for asset management or cost-cutting measures, but for expertise, management tactics, and EOR technologies.[35] The UAE so far has fallen far short of the Saudi level of adoption of advanced management and development techniques and technology.

The UAE is developing the infrastructure needed for an increased oil production capacity in reaction to the rapidly expanding Asian market and the abundance of opportunities for UAE investors to make huge profits by securing their export share of the increasingly high demand in the Pacific Rim. The UAE is also looking to expand its portfolio by buying into utility and gas companies overseas, as well as forming partnerships with a foreign firm and buying into the liquefied petroleum gas market.[36]

The UAE's overall political stability seems good, but there are areas of uncertainty. Sheik Zayed of Abu Dhabi died on November 2, 2004. Though the transition to his son, Khalifah, has been smooth, it is still unclear if he has the ability to keep the Al-Nahayan family together while maintaining the support to the other six families ruling the emirates. Zayed left behind 19 sons from many wives, and the competition for power between them might threaten the stability of largest emirate, Abu Dhabi, and eventually the union.

Some experts have argued that Khalifah lacks the leadership skills of his father, and that he will be overshadowed by his younger half-brother,

Mohammad, whom his father named as deputy crown prince in 2003.[37] Mohammad bin Zayed is also the chief of staff of the UAE Armed Forces and is competing with the crown prince of Dubai, Mohammad bin Rashed Al-Maktoom, who is also the defense minister. Though the friction has been kept civil during Sheik Zayed's life, it remains uncertain how the two Mohammads' relationship is developing following the passing of Zayed.

The competition within and between the families was apparent in June 2003 when the ruler of Ras Al-Khaimah replaced Crown Prince Khalid, who opposed the United States–led war in Iraq with another son. Crown Prince Khalid and his supporters objected to the decision, and the situation almost became violent, which led the government in Abu Dhabi to send an armored personnel carrier to protect the ruler of Ras Al-Khaimah and break up the protest.[38]

Yemen: Although Yemen is making progress toward internal stability, it has a long history of civil war and violence. It also has a large and rapidly growing population of more than 20 million, which its economy cannot support. Only remittances from workers overseas and foreign aid allow the nation to function. This economic and demographic instability, coupled with a long history of tolerating the presence of extremist and terrorist movements when they do not directly threaten the regime, makes Yemen a potential threat to both Oman and Saudi Arabia.

The Yemeni government actively courts foreign oil companies, especially because most of the major international firms pulled out of the country in the middle and late 1990s due to a violent civil war, unattractive exploration and production contractual conditions, and a low success rate in new hydrocarbon discoveries.

In 2001, improvements to the terms of foreign investment were passed that allow more flexibility in contracts as well as the ability to negotiate contract extensions on a case-by-case basis and amend restrictive legislation. However, the government has been inconsistent in its reform process, as exemplified by its 2001 cancellation of the Aden refinery rebuilding process, which was initially scheduled for privatization but now is subject only to a vague plan of intention to sell partial stakes to private firms in the future.

Yemen seeks to become an LNG producer, but its future in the industry has looked bleak since a massive pullout in 2002 by several companies scheduled to build up its LNG infrastructure. Another obstacle to its becoming a major LNG producer is competition from regional powers like Iran and Oman, which both have more advanced pipeline infrastructures and more investment contracts and offers to expand their existing networks. Industry inconsistencies, coupled with a resurgence of rioting in August 2005 over a doubling of national fuel prices, make Yemen's future appear much bleaker than those of its regional counterparts.

Strategically, Yemen is the wild card in the southern Gulf. In strict terms, it is not a southern Gulf power. It has coasts and islands on the Indian Ocean and Red Sea, and it occupies a strategic position at the Bab el Mandab—the narrow strait controlling the entrance to the Red Sea that every ship passing through the Suez Canal must traverse. It does, however, share borders with Oman. Though Yemen has resolved its border disputes with Oman and Saudi Arabia, there has been a long history of tension between Yemen and its neighbors. Yemen sponsored a violent Marxist insurgent movement and provided it with military support and sanctuary during Oman's Dhofar rebellion.

In addition, there is a long history of clashes on the Saudi–Yemeni border. And smuggling from Yemen to Saudi Arabia—including the supply of arms and explosives for Islamic terrorists—is a continuing problem.

Egypt: Egypt is currently a small exporter of energy, but its oil export revenues are one of its top four main foreign exchange earners (along with tourism, Suez Canal fees, and worker remittances from abroad). The EIA estimates that the country produced 0.594 mmbpd of oil in 2004, a drastic drop from the all-time high of nearly 0.922 mmbpd in 1996. Egyptian oil production comes from four main areas: the Gulf of Suez (about 50 percent), the Western Desert, the Eastern Desert, and the Sinai Peninsula. The Egyptian Ministry of Petroleum estimates that it has 66.0 tcf of gas.

Despite recent declines, Egypt is hoping that exploration activity funded by current high fuel prices will discover sufficient oil in coming years to return crude oil production to a maintainable level, near 0.80 mmbpd. So far, exploration and production-boosting projects, especially near the Gulf of Suez and Western Desert, have proven fruitful. A revamping of the Suez Canal intended to cut down transit times may also prove lucrative.

Jordan: Jordan has no meaningful oil resources of its own, making its importance in Middle Eastern energy largely political. It relies completely on imported oil for most of its needs (about 0.160 mmbpd in 2004); and during the 2003 Iraq War, almost all of this oil came at a discounted rate from Iraq. Before the war, Jordan's $500 million worth of oil imports from Iraq was permitted by the United Nations under a special dispensation from the general UN embargo on Iraq, largely because Jordan did not have the use of an operating pipeline, requiring all its oil imports to be shipped in by truck.

Due to drastic changes in Jordan's oil supply—and its loss of cheap, subsidized oil from Iraq—it has pushed forward with plans for the exploration and development of its own oil potential, which is largely unknown as of yet. To help attract foreign investment to this new and expensive endeavor, the Jordanian government has plans to privatize its oil sector and possibly to burn shale for electricity.

The Jordan Petroleum Refining Corporation, which owns the only refinery in the country, located at Zarqa, is currently studying its options for a possible modernization program. The current facility has an operating capacity of 0.0904 mmbpd and was originally designed to produce a product mix skewed toward heavy fuel oil for electricity generation. However, the current domestic market is in need of additional gasoline and diesel fuel, because natural gas is now used for the majority of electric power plants.[39]

Israel-Palestine: Although Israel has historically relied on Egypt, the North Sea, West Africa, and Mexico to supply its energy needs, it now reportedly imports a majority of its oil from former Soviet countries, such as Russia and the Caspian Sea nations. Its most notable gas purchases come from Egypt, which in 2005 agreed to provide Israel with 60 billion cubic feet per year for 15 years, marking a large step toward political progress as well.[40] Israel's Petroleum Commission estimates that the country could contain up to 5 billion barrels of oil located under gas reserves; however, only 20 million barrels are believed to be extractable.

Gas has also been discovered in areas that lie in Palestinian territorial waters off the Gaza Strip. The EIA reports that British Gas (BG), which first struck gas in this area with its Gaza Marine-1 well in August 1999, has signed a 25-year contract to explore for gas and set up a gas network under the Palestinian Authority. In December 2000, BG successfully completed drilling a second gas well in waters off the Gaza shore. The drilling confirmed findings from the Marine-1 well, which had flowed at 37 million cubic feet per day, indicating possible reserves of about 1.4 tcf. BG plans to invest $400 million in its offshore Gaza gas finds, which could be used to supply Israel, along with other sources.

These plans, however, have so far been blocked by the Israeli government, for a variety of reasons. There is particular Israeli apprehension over the al-Khoury family, which owns shares in the Consolidated Contractors Company, which in turn holds a minority share in the Marine fields. BG has engaged in considerable lobbying to persuade the Israeli government to purchase gas from the Gazan Marine fields, an agreement that is necessary for BG to consider the venture commercially viable and begin developing the fields. An earlier BG proposal involved setting up a barter agreement, under which Palestine would receive electricity in exchange for providing Israel with natural gas, thereby avoiding the exchange of money altogether.[41]

After a stall in negotiations through mid-2005, there has been a significant renewal of interest in the offshore Gaza gas fields, due to the Israeli withdrawal from the Gaza Strip in August 2005. In July 2005, the Palestinian Authority and Egypt agreed to arrange a protocol for sales of offshore Gaza gas to Egypt, with long-term plans to export LNG to world markets.[42] This option, which was introduced with a threat from BG to bypass Israel completely in negotiations over commercialization, sparked a sudden reconsideration by the Israeli government. Prime Minister Ariel Sharon signed a preliminary agreement with BG in September 2005 to import offshore Gaza gas. However, disagreements remain over whether Israel will pay in cash or in electricity for the imported gas, and no contracts had been finalized as of October 2005.[43]

Syria: Syrian oil production dropped sharply in 2003 when illegal imports from Iraq were cut off. In addition, its oil development has been politicized and inefficient, and its economic reforms, including those related to oil, have either failed or moved too slowly in virtually every respect. Without significant new discoveries in the next few years, oil officials predict that the country could become a net oil importer by the end of 2005.

Although Syria's oil exports have had little impact on world energy balances, they have been critical to its economy, accounting for 55 to 60 percent of its total export earnings. It currently exports Syrian Light, a blend of light and sweet crudes produced primarily from the Deir ez-Zour and Ash Sham fields, and heavy Suwaidiyah crude produced from the Soudie and Jebisseh fields. The country also exports fuel oil and other products, which used to include oil sent illegally from Iraq; but this dropped sharply after the March 2003 war. Syria is a member of the Organization of Arab Petroleum Exporting Countries, although not of OPEC.

Syria is attempting to reform in its energy sector by using, for example, intensified oil exploration and production efforts, and by switching to natural gas–fired electric power plants to maximize revenue from oil exports. However, its relationship with Iraq and the United States is on the decline, and it has failed to take its security situation seriously or make a genuine effort at long-term political and economic reform.

Key Strategic Challenges

Countries in the Middle East face long-term strategic challenges as well as short-term to midterm uncertainty. The risk premium of these uncertainties is hard to quantify, but the following are the key strategic challenges that the Gulf and the greater Middle East face, which have direct and indirect effects on the energy market:

- *Internal threats from extremists:* Saudi Arabia has experienced attacks since the May 2003 bombing. The Kingdom's forces have proved their ability to deal with this threat. However, the question remains: Can the other southern Gulf states withstand such attacks?

- *Asymmetric threats toward the Strait of Hormuz and oil facilities:* The security challenges to the Gulf countries are to prevent attacks against oil infrastructure and reduce the damage when they occur.

- *Instability in Iraq:* The uncertain outcome in Iraq and the possible spillover of insurgency into the neighboring states remain a real threat to stability in the rest of the region. Cross-border infiltrations by fighters have been reported, but currently only crossing into Iraq. Will these fighters go back to their countries? Do the governments of these countries have a plan to deal with them? Or will they become like the "Afghan Arabs"?

- *The "glitter factor" with regard to regional status:* Rivalries and past tensions between the southern Gulf states prevented serious efforts to develop joint capabilities and interoperability. At the same time, a number of states limited their military efforts because of the fear of coups. The result was that the southern Gulf states largely preferred de facto dependence on U.S. and British power projection forces over effective regional and national military efforts.

- *Lack of economic diversification:* The Gulf economies continue to be highly dependent on oil. With no exception, the Gulf countries lack a vibrant private sector. This adds to the economic uncertainty due to the volatility of the oil market and the high dependence of state budgets on oil revenues.

- *Fiscal and debt crunches:* Many countries in the region, despite great oil wealth, have faced budget derelicts, large sovereign debts, slow privatization campaigns, and lagging financial sectors. Such stagnation tends to crowd out valuable foreign and domestic private investment, which is much needed to create jobs and build a vibrant private sector.

- *High unemployment rates:* Estimates for unemployment are unreliable, but most countries in the Middle East have a large number of unemployed citizens. Moreover, the southern Gulf States continue to rely heavily on foreign labor. Saudization, Bahrainization,

Emaritization, and the like have shown little success in the past decade.

- *Reforming educational systems:* Part of solving the unemployment problem is reforming the educational system to better prepare students for a competitive job market. Young people without a job tend to blame the situation on the regime and become a recruitment target for extremist causes.

- *The demographic "time bomb":* In most of the Middle East, more than 50 percent of the population is under the age of 30 years. This has many implications. First, it deepens the unemployment problem. Most countries are adding more people to the job market than the market can employ. Second, it adds fiscal constraints to government programs and social entitlements, including health care and public education, which further complicates the fiscal situation of their economies. Third, the population distribution is such that most people are young, unemployed, and the perfect target for extremist recruitment.

- *Iran's WMD program:* The southern Gulf States will have to find a way to deal with a nuclear Iran by building a missile defense shield, acquiring their own WMD, or relying on the United States' power projection in the Gulf.

- *The ongoing Israeli–Palestinian conflict:* The Gulf oil policy and the Palestinian issue have been kept separate by both the United States and the Gulf countries. The leadership in the Gulf, however, is facing pressure from its population to use its oil political capital to help the Palestinian cause.

Production Risks and Developments

A combination of low oil prices and geopolitical uncertainties limited investment in the energy sector in the Middle East until the recovery of oil prices began in the late 1990s. As a result, some of the region's oil infrastructure is aging. Countries in the Gulf have spent a lot of money on internal security and on social and economic programs, and some have spent less money on upgrading and expanding their oil production and export facilities as well as their downstream operations.

The shift toward high oil prices seems to have provided the necessary incentives for new investments. There are, however, production and resource risks in the Middle East, even if the region's political and military risks can be minimized and investment capital becomes available:

- *Natural depletion rates:* Some analysts argue that the depletion rates of major oil fields are higher than reported. The implications are that current reserve estimates of production capacity may not also be what are being reported.

- *Depletion of Iran's oil fields:* Iran's oil fields are estimated to have a natural depletion of 0.20 to 0.25 mmbpd. These fields need to be upgraded, and it is estimated that the country's oil infrastructure needs as much as $1 billion in foreign investment to reach 5.0 mmbpd by 2009.

- *Iran's large subsidies:* It is estimated that the Iranian government pays large subsidies totaling more than $3 billion a year, resulting in large wastes and inefficiencies.

- *Intense water management systems:* Oil companies in the Middle East, and for that matter in most places, have used intense water injection to postpone natural depletion. Water management, however, can cause damage to the oil fields and may cause the fields to collapse.

- *Major oil fields that may have "peaked":* The Gulf has a dozen giant and supergiant fields. Though the published data regarding depletion and reserves are uncertain, some of these fields are old and their upstream infrastructure has aged. Are there other fields large enough to replace these giant fields?

- *Dependence on giant and supergiant fields:* Oil officials in the region claim that these fields are huge, and even if they have aged, they are larger than any other fields we have seen and it will be a long time before they are out of oil. Though it is true that these fields are huge and may have a long way to go before they run out of oil, producing nations are dependent on the health of these fields.

- *Insufficiency of vertical wells:* When oil fields mature, vertical wells are not enough to extract oil, and therefore horizontal wells or maximum recovery contact may be required to produce oil.

- *Politicization of reserves and capacity:* Oil reserves are seen as signaling strategic importance. Some experts have argued that countries inflate their oil reserves as a political tool against their neighbors and outside powers.

- *Little spare production capacity:* With the exception of Saudi Arabia, in 2005, the other Gulf and Middle Eastern countries had no spare capacity. This requires large foreign and private domestic investment in technology and in capacity expansion programs—given that the current surge in demand is not expected to cool off anytime soon.

- *Loss of valuable Iraqi reservoir data:* Following the invasion of Iraq, experts believe, many valuable data were looted from the Iraqi oil fields and the Ministry of Oil's regional buildings.

- *Iraq's labor force:* Workers in the Iraqi oil sector lack the training to develop and modernize the energy industry due to sanctions and the instability of the postconflict situation.

AFRICA

Africa is becoming a steadily more important oil producer and exporter. Figure 5.5 shows current estimates of African oil reserves. Africa's proven reserves were estimated to be 112.2 billion barrels in 2004 (9.4 percent of the world's total proven reserves). This is nearly double what the continent was estimated to have in 1994 (roughly 65 billion barrels of proven reserves). In 2003, a U.S. energy task force headed by Vice President Dick Cheney projected that Africa's oil sector would become the fastest growing in the world.[44] During the past few years, this projection has been proved correct; Africa has been the fastest growing region in discoveries and production. African production capacity was 8.6 mmbpd in 2002. According to the EIA forecast issued in 2005 and shown in figure 5.6, its production capacity will nearly double by 2025 (15.4 mmbpd for the high case and 16.4 mmbpd for the reference case).

Figure 5.5
Africa Proven, Known, Undiscovered Oil Reserves (billion barrels)

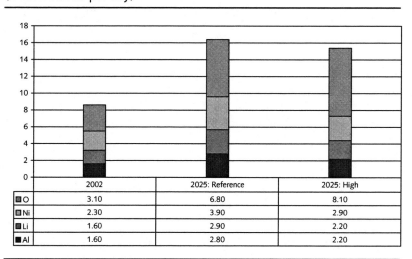

	Algeria	Angola	Cameroon	Gabon	Libya	Nigeria	Republic of Congo	Sudan	Tunisia
Kn	18.28	6.78	1.24	4.17	38.90	33.20	2.50	0.00	1.52
Un	7.73	14.52	1.53	8.18	8.27	37.62	5.80	0.77	2.18
Pr	11.80	8.80	0.20	2.30	39.10	35.30	1.80	6.30	0.60

Source: Adapted by the authors from BP, *Statistical Review of World Energy 2005,* and
   the *U.S. Geological Survey 2000.*
Note: Kn = known; Un = undiscovered; Pr = proven.

Figure 5.6
U.S. EIA Estimates of Africa Oil Production Capacity
(million barrels per day)

	2002	2025: Reference	2025: High
O	3.10	6.80	8.10
Ni	2.30	3.90	2.90
Li	1.60	2.90	2.20
Al	1.60	2.80	2.20

Source: Adapted by the authors from U.S. Energy Information Administration,
   International Energy Outlook 2005.
Note: O = Other; Ni = Nigeria; Li = Libya; Al =·Algeria

West Africa's share of the world's total, including unproven reserves, now seems to have reached 7 percent. The Gulf of Guinea has 33.8 billion barrels of proven reserves, which is relatively small compared with those of the Middle East, which has 733.9 billion barrels of proven reserves. In addition, production costs in the region of the Economic Community of West African States are higher because the majority of the oil reserves are offshore.[45]

National Developments

Nigeria, a member of OPEC, has the largest reserves (known, undiscovered, and proven) on the continent, including approximately 35.3 billion barrels of proven reserves. In addition, according to the *U.S. Geological Survey 2000* (hereafter *USGS 2000*), Nigeria has about 37.62 billion barrels of undiscovered oil.

Nigeria is the largest West African producer, and the fifth largest exporter to the United States. Fully half its exports of 2.5 mmbpd flow to the United States. The Gulf of Guinea as a whole currently supplies 15 percent of U.S. oil and, according to the U.S. National Intelligence Council, may supply 25 percent by 2015. In the next five years, one in five new barrels of oil on the global market will come from the region.[46]

Some experts argue that the ability to exploit West African oil and gas reserves should not be overestimated. Geostrategic risks—including revolutions, violence, and corruption—have limited the productive potential of these reserves. And border disputes have slowed the process of developing offshore oil fields in West Africa.

Interethnic strife and violence in the Niger Delta, including kidnapping, sabotage, and attacks on oil facilities, have caused production and supply disruptions. For example:

- In March 2003, ChevronTexaco and Shell moved some of their staffs off location and suspended their production in the Niger Delta, which caused Nigerian production to drop by 13 percent or 0.266 mmbpd.[47]

- In June 2005, the U.S. consulate in Lagos was closed for several days due to an Internet terror threat, supposedly posted by Osama bin Laden, that marked the country for "liberation."[48]

- On September 23, 2005, the Nigerian radical separatist group People's Volunteer Force issued a statement, in which it threatened, "We will kill every iota of oil operations in the Niger Delta. We will destroy anything and everything. We will challenge our enemies in our territory and we shall feed them to the vultures." The threat came after the Nigerian authorities arrested the group's leader, Mujahid Dokubo-Asari, on allegations of treason. The government of Nigeria announced that it had deployed 900 extra police officers. Following the statement, ChevronTexaco and Shell shut their oil facilities in the Niger Delta. The two Chevron stations that were shut down produced 0.027 mmbpd.[49]

Nigerian exports to the United States have been affected by this instability. During 2002, oil exports to the United States from Nigeria decreased by 6.27 percent. Regional and energy experts have argued that increasing U.S. reliance on West African oil means increasing the U.S. vulnerability to the region's instability.[50]

Some humanitarian organizations have argued that the growth in the national energy sectors has hampered balanced economic and social development in Nigeria and other African oil-exporting states. Catholic Relief Services, for example, has reported that African countries where oil was discovered a few decades ago—such as Gabon, Angola, and Nigeria—had lower rates of economic development, growth, and poverty reduction that those without oil.[51] Part of this stagnation can be attributed to oil-related corruption and a lack of transparency. In addition, governments in such countries have relied on oil revenues to support their state budgets and have done little to liberalize and diversify their economies away from the oil sector.[52]

Angola has the second largest undiscovered reserves in Africa, roughly 14.52 billion barrels of oil in addition to 8.8 billion barrels of proven reserves. Though the Angolan civil war is over, oil development faces other problems. In 2003, the International Monetary Fund found that $1 billion of the Angolan government's $5 billion budget goes missing every year. Moreover, Global Witness, a human rights organization based in the United Kingdom, made the claim that the money from oil contracts—paid to Angolan government officials, including

President José Eduardo dos Santos—helped extend Angola's civil war.[53]

Sudan's oil industry has shown progress in the past several years. It is estimated to have 6.30 billion barrels of proven reserves and 0.77 billion barrels of undiscovered reserves. During the past decade, Sudan's oil production and exports have increased rapidly. Its production averaged 0.270 mmbpd in 2003 and 0.343 mmbpd in 2004; and according to Sudanese government claims, it could reach 0.50 mmbpd by the end of 2005. The EIA estimates that Sudan's oil production could reach 0.750 mmbpd by the end of 2006, if the same level of progress is sustained.[54]

Despite progress in Sudan's energy sector, it continues to suffer from a low-intensity civil war between the Muslims in the north and the Christians in the south that has killed an estimated 2 million Sudanese since 1983. In May 2004, the parties signed the Marchakos Protocol, which in part outlined the division of oil revenues in half between the north and the south. In August 2005, John Garang, the leader of the Sudan People Liberation Front and the vice president of the country, died in a helicopter clash. His death led to riots in the country and added to the uncertainties surrounding the peace accord between the north and south.[55]

In addition, ethnic strife and instability continue in Darfur, where an estimated 10,000 to 30,000 people have been killed and as many as 1 million displaced as refugees. The UN Security Council has threatened to take action against the oil industry and the government in Khartoum; in February 2005, it called the situation in Darfur genocide.[56]

The United States had made efforts to improve stability in the region. It was reported that the U.S. European Command was talking to leaders in West Africa to increase cooperation to protect the oil facilities in Nigeria, Angola, Cameroon, Guinea, and Ghana. The United States held a meeting in October 2004 to discuss energy security with regional leaders. Western Africa supplies roughly 14 percent of the United States' imports, which is nearly double what it was 20 years ago, and some experts predict that if the same rate of offshore discovery continues, the proportion of U.S. imports from Africa could rise to 20 percent in the next decade.[57]

Given the importance of the West African region, the United States is also trying to curb corruption there. Colonel Mike Anderson, the chief policy planner for the U.S. European Command, has said that the United States is working with West African leaders to put in place anti-corruption measures; but he has also said of these efforts, "It's a tough nut to crack there."[58]

As for current and future production and exports, Algeria and Nigeria have dominated past oil production in Africa, but figure 5.6 shows that the EIA forecasts that other African countries, presumably in West Africa, will increase their production capacity from 3.10 mmbpd in 2002 to between 6.80 and 8.10 mmbpd, depending on oil prices. Nigeria, Algeria, and Libya will see some increases in their productive capacity. Figure 5.6 shows that the EIA estimated that their capacity would increase from 5.5 mmbpd in 2002 to 9.6 mmbpd in the reference case and 7.3 mmbpd in the high-price case in 2025.

The problem with such estimates is that demand-driven modeling again ignores actual country plans and the risks imposed by regional political instability. In the real world, actual output could be much lower for political investment and management reasons, or much higher as poor nations seek to maximize oil imports by any means possible.

Key Strategic Challenges

The geopolitical risks in Africa are as complex—if not more so—as those in the Middle East. Ethnic tensions, government corruption, and border disputes compound the uncertainty of the energy sector in Africa and the global oil market. As is the case with the other oil-producing regions, quantifying geopolitical risks is impossible, but the following are the major strategic challenges faced by the continent's producing nations:

- *The HIV/AIDS epidemic:* The continent of Africa continues to be threatened by the AIDS virus. Between 1981 and 2003, HIV/AIDS killed 20 million people. Almost 1,600 children die of AIDS worldwide, and at least 90 percent of them are African. This represents social, economic, health, and humanitarian crises.

- *Ethnic and tribal conflicts:* The ongoing conflict in Darfur, the low-intensity civil war in Algeria, the ethnic division in Zimbabwe, and the fragile peace in Rwanda have contributed to the ongoing uncertainty and instability in Africa. A long-term realistic strategy must be put in place to deal with them.

- *Nigeria's fragile stability:* Muslim–Christian relations in Nigeria are tenuous, and their deterioration can be dangerous to stability in West Africa. The lack of strong political, economic, and judicial institutions compounds the religious strife and adds to the uncertainty in the countries on the Gulf of Guinea.

- *Instability in Angola:* Since the end of the civil war, the Angolan government has made some improvement in its control over the country. It is still unclear, however, whether Luanda has made enough reforms in the areas of good governance, security, and the energy sector.

- *Transit and training ground for terrorism:* Some extremist movements have found a safe haven in East Africa due to the failure of the region's governments to control their borders and due to its proximity to the Gulf and Saudi Arabia. Outside powers must help governments deal with this phenomenon through training programs, intelligence sharing, and assistance in patrolling their shores.

- *Illicit small arms smuggling:* Countries such as the Democratic Republic of Congo, Sierra Leone, Angola, and parts of Nigeria and Liberia have also experienced internal conflicts in recent years. Small arms in the hands of warlords have caused a lot of damage to human life and infrastructure. Since the start of the "global war on terrorism," security services have turned their attention to transnational terrorist organizations in West Africa and their relation to illegal diamonds and arms smuggling.

- *Transparent and accountable governments:* The African continent continues to lack good governance and is plagued by corruption, as in Zimbabwe and Liberia. Nigeria has announced programs to reform its government and improve transparency. But it remains unclear whether the Nigerian government is following through on its plans.

- *Coups and military takeovers:* Countries in Africa are plagued with insurgency and coups. On August 3, 2005, the Mauritanian army ousted President Maaouya Ould Sid'Ahmed Taya, and the military rulers appointed a new civilian government and declared that it will hold elections within two years.

- *Effective regional security forces:* The African Union lacks any well-trained, deployable, and effective regional security forces. Such forces are needed to stop ethnic strife, as in Rwanda, or to calm political unrest, as in Liberia.

- *Gulf of Guinea border disputes:* The countries on the Gulf of Guinea have argued throughout history over their land and sea borders. There have been signs of success in peacefully resolving some of these disputes, but many others remain unresolved.

- *Transnational terrorism:* Regional experts argue that weak government, poverty, and ethnic strife can create fertile ground where transnational terrorist organizations can operate and recruit for their cause. Groups such as Al Qaeda are operating in Africa, especially in East Africa. It remains uncertain how well established they are in countries in West Africa such as Nigeria.

Production Risks and Developments

In addition to the geostrategic risks, Africa faces other petroleum development problems. African oil reserves are often offshore and costly to extract. At the same time, recent discoveries and production developments are changing the face of African oil. Key recent developments and production challenges in the oil sector include the following:

- *Highest rate of discovery in the world:* During the past five years, West Africa has seen the highest rate of discovery in the world, mostly in the Gulf of Guinea. The majority of the growth has come from Nigeria and Angola.

- *Angola's production level:* According to the EIA, by 2008, Angola's oil production is estimated to reach 2.8 mmbpd. The country is still recovering, however, from 27 years of civil war, and its oil industry continues to suffer from a lack of transparency, corruption, and the misuse of its oil revenues by government officials.

- *Lack of economic development:* This growth, however, has come at the cost of necessary economic development and poverty reduction programs. As mentioned above, the countries with higher rates of oil discovery have had the lowest economic liberalization and poverty reduction rates.

- *Lack of foreign investment:* There has been an inflow of foreign investment; however, it has gone mostly to West African countries. Central and North African countries have seen limited investment, especially in the area of upgrading current infrastructure and exploration to replenish natural depletion in existing oil fields.

- *Lack of transparency:* Nongovernmental organizations have reported cases of corruption by oil officials. For example, the World Bank reported that 80 percent of the oil revenue in Nigeria went to 1 percent of the population, despite the fact that 70 percent of the population is living in poverty.

- *Libya's dated energy infrastructure:* Due to sanctions and mismanagement, Libyan oil infrastructure is aging and has not been upgraded since the 1970s. Lacks of technological capabilities and sound transportation systems have prevented Libya from increasing its production capacity.

- *Deep offshore reserves and facilities:* Most of the new discoveries in West Africa are offshore and in the deep sea. Though these reserves and facilities are removed from any social conflict, pipelines and onshore oil facilities continue to be vulnerable to rebel attacks. Moreover, offshore reserves have higher production costs, requiring advanced technologies and a higher level of foreign investment.

- *Rebel attacks:* Violent clashes between ethnic groups in the Niger Delta region have caused enough insecurity for some oil companies to evacuate their operations from Nigeria. Rebel groups have attacked and sabotaged oil installations. Algeria is another example; the Algerian military estimates that 400 militants or terrorists are currently residing in the country. In 2001, approximately 1,100 people were killed in clashes with insurgents.

- *Environmental damage of oil exploration and production:* According to the EIA, there has been "chronic release of oil" into the shipping ports, which has significant effects on the environment. This problem, however, is often ignored.

- *Strikes and labor disputes:* Labor disputes have caused disruption to oil production in Nigeria. Strikes, tax laws, and corruption continue to limit much needed foreign and private investment in the oil sector in Central and West Africa.

- *Sudan's lagging oil industry:* In 2005, Sudan's oil production level was roughly 0.50 mmbpd, and it is estimated to have a potential to reach 0.75 mmbpd by 2006. The tenuous peace agreement in the south and the unrest in Darfur continue to plague the country and have prevented the flow of foreign investment into Sudan's oil industry.

ASIA AND THE PACIFIC

As figure 5.7 shows, the Asia-Pacific region has the lowest oil reserves of any region. In 2004, BP reported that the region had 41.1 billion barrels of proven reserves. It also has some undiscovered reserves. According to the *USGS 2000*, Asia contains roughly 32.064 billion barrels of undiscovered reserves. Figure 5.8 shows the region also has low levels of production, which are estimated to increase from 7.5 mmbpd in 2002 to only between 8.7 and 9.0 mmbpd in 2025.

National Developments

China has the largest oil reserves in the region, with 48.5 billion barrels of known reserves. Its production capacity in 2005 was 3.6 mmbpd; this capacity has seen little growth and is not expected to grow significantly in the future. The EIA projects that by 2020; Chinese production capacity could reach 3.8 mmbpd in the high-price case, or remain

Figure 5.7
Asia Pacific Proven, Known, Undiscovered Oil Reserves (billion barrels)

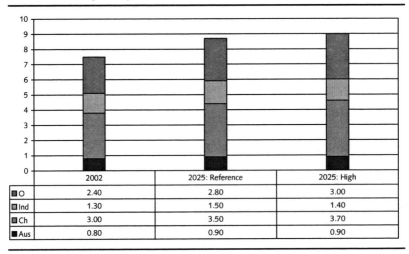

	Australia	Brunei	China	India	Indonesia	Malaysia	Papua New Guinea	Thailand	Vietnam
Kn	5.56	4.09	48.46	10.98	22.42	7.18	?	0.00	9.00
Un	4.98	1.80	12.12	2.56	7.44	3.04	?	0.10	0.04
Pr	4.00	1.10	17.10	5.60	4.70	4.30	0.40	0.50	3.00

Source: Adapted by the authors from BP, *Statistical Review of World Energy 2005*, and the *U.S. Geological Survey 2000*.
Note: Kn = known; Un = undiscovered; Pr = proven.

Figure 5.8
U.S. EIA Estimates of Asia-Pacific Oil Production Capacity
(million barrels per day)

	2002	2025: Reference	2025: High
O	2.40	2.80	3.00
Ind	1.30	1.50	1.40
Ch	3.00	3.50	3.70
Aus	0.80	0.90	0.90

Source: Adapted by the authors from U.S. Energy Information Administration, *International Energy Outlook 2005*.
Note: O = Other; Ind = Indonesia; Ch = China; Aus = Australia.

at 3.6 mmbpd in the reference case. All of China's production is sold domestically in addition to the 3.0 to 4.0 mmbpd of oil it imports.

Indonesia is the only Asian country that is a member of OPEC. It has 22.4 billion barrels of known reserves, 4.7 billion barrels of proven reserves, and 7.4 billion barrels of undiscovered reserves. Though these numbers are small, Indonesia has played a major role in OPEC in the past. Its production, however, declined in 2003 and 2004 due to natural depletion and aging oil fields. Its oil industry is in need of investment and further exploration to replace this decline.

The EIA forecasts that Indonesia's oil production capacity will stay at the same level in 2025 as it was in 2001: 1.5 mmbpd. This would make Indonesia an oil importer and not an exporter. In August 2005, the Indonesian government announced that the country was a net oil importer in the second quarter of 2005. During the same period, the country's imports averaged 0.080 mmbpd. Indonesia's OPEC quota is 1.45 mmbpd, but it produced only 0.94 mmbpd in June 2005.[59]

According the EIA, the new Indonesian oil field, Cepu, which is estimated to hold at least 600 million barrels of oil reserves, is being developed by ExxonMobil in partnership with Pertamina. But the partners cannot agree on profit sharing or on extending ExxonMobil's technical assistance beyond 2020. Despite the 2001 legislation that attempted to limit the company's monopoly power in the upstream business, corruption charges against Pertamina continue to surface.[60]

With the exception of India, the rest of Asia consumes a growing amount of energy with little petroleum production. India's oil consumption has grown rapidly in the past decade. In 2003, its average production was 0.819 mmbpd, leaving it with a net 1.4 mmbpd imports. It is trying to decrease its dependence on foreign sources of energy, so it is expanding exploration, has ended price controls, and is planning to build a strategic petroleum storage capacity.

Japan lacks large domestic petroleum reserves. According to the EIA, Japan contains only 59 million barrels of proven reserves. Its domestic production is minimal, but it is the third largest consumer of energy after the United States and China. In 2004, Japan consumed 5.288 mmbpd.

To compensate for this deficit, Japanese companies have been active overseas, including in Indonesia, the Gulf, and Russia. The loss of drilling rights in the Saudi portion of the Saudi–Kuwaiti Neutral Zone was a major disappointment. The concession, which ended in February 2000, was producing 0.82 mmbpd for Japan's Arab Oil Company. The loss of the Neutral Zone deal meant the loss of nearly a fifth of Japan's oil consumption.[61]

The Russian Far East is another potential source of energy for Japan, and the Japanese have proposed the Nakhodka pipeline, which would extend from Siberia to the Pacific coast, with direct access to Japan. In mid-2004, Japan offered to finance up to $10 billion of the pipeline cost.[62]

Japan is competing with China as the main guarantor of the Siberian oil from the Nakhodka Pipeline, and the two nations have been engaged in a bidding war for several years over the pipeline's route, the amount of government subsidies available to promote their respective offers to Russia, and the feasibility of drilling in the Siberian region. Differing opinions exist as to the actual amount of proven reserves in Siberia, and extreme winter temperatures make it difficult to drill in the frozen ground to complete exploration, drilling, and pipeline construction.[63]

Two possible routes for the Nakhodka Pipeline have been discussed, which would transport 1.0 mmbpd from Siberia to the rapidly growing East Asian oil market. The China National Petroleum Corporation and Russia's Yukos Oil have agreed to transport 1.0 mmbpd of crude oil from Anagarsk, Siberia, to join the existing pipeline network at Daqing, which would enable virtually all the oil to flow into the Chinese market. Japan's $10 billion offer came after an alternative plan backed by Russia's Transneft was proposed, which would create a spur leading to the Pacific port of Nakhodka. Transneft will begin construction of the first phase of the pipeline to Skovordino, approximately 50 miles from the Chinese border, as early as the end of 2005, despite the lack of an agreement on the final destination of the pipeline.[64] Russia likely may continue to entertain the price war between China and Japan, and it can ultimately sign an agreement with the highest bidder.

Key Strategic Challenges

Given the volume of exports by Asian countries such as Japan, South Korea, China, India, and Taiwan, a disruption of petroleum supply to these countries would have a major influence on both their economies and the many other economies that depend on imports from them.

Aside from the risk of another Asian economic crisis, most of the other long-term strategic risks are subregional. As mentioned above, the Asia-Pacific region is a net importer of oil, but it is an important oil-consuming region.

China, India, and Pakistan, which are all nuclear powers, have ongoing strategic disputes and tensions. North Korea continues to pose a threat to its neighbor and may have nuclear weapons. The two most populous countries in the world, China and India, are rising economic and military powers with uncertain future ambitions and growing needs for petroleum imports.

The following risks could have a major future influence on the stability of the region and the global oil market:

- *North Korea's nuclear program:* It is likely that the North Korean regime has at least one nuclear weapon. A confrontation with North Korea could destabilize the region and force Japan to acquire its own nuclear weapons.

- *China and Taiwan:* China's ambitions toward Taiwan are clear and unlikely to change anytime soon. With China's rising military and economic power, the recent expressed U.S. unhappiness with Taiwan's quest for independence, and the complexity of United States–China relations, it is unclear what the American response to Chinese aggression against Taiwan would be.

- *India and Pakistan's nuclear standoff:* These two nuclear rivals have been in stances of confrontation for more than 50 years. The situation is complicated by any instability in the region and the possible transfer of nuclear weapons into the hands of transnational terrorist organizations.

- *Terrorism and counterterrorism:* Counterterrorism efforts in Afghanistan, Pakistan, Indonesia, the Philippines, and other Southeast Asian countries have proven effective. However, terrorist organizations may have well-established cells, and the war against such organizations is far from over.

- *China's rise:* Experts argue that the rise of China could be a major strategic challenge to the United States in the Asia-Pacific region. However, it is becoming a key U.S. economic partner and a major economic power, and its economy is a key factor in world oil demand.

- *India's rise:* India's economic progress in the past decade has been miraculous. Most recently, its energy demand has surged. Moreover, it has been on the receiving end of much U.S. corporate outsourcing. But poverty, HIV/AIDS, and ethnic clashes continue to be long-term challenges.

Production Risks and Developments

Asian oil production suffers from natural depletion and a lack of investment in the exploration and production sector. The lack of new discoveries is largely due to limited reserves but is also affected by a lack of investment, the ruggedness of the terrain, and strict environmental laws.

The security of oil facilities and ethnic disputes are currently only limited problems in Asia, largely affecting only Indonesia. Territorial disputes and large-scale wars could, however, significantly affect future energy supply. The following production developments in the Asia-Pacific region affect its energy supply and security:

- *Territorial disputes:* China, the Philippines, Malaysia, Vietnam, Indonesia, Thailand, and Brunei continue to contest the ownership of offshore natural resources in the South China Sea. Though the parties have agreed to shelve their disputes and avoid confrontation, the economic development of these resources remains limited, contributing to the uncertain nature of energy resources in the region.

- *Rugged terrain:* According to the EIA, pre-tertiary basins in eastern Indonesia contain large but unproven oil reserves. The ruggedness of the terrain, however, has limited exploration, and it is uncertain if these reserves exist or if they can become productive. Terrain is similarly a problem for Russia's Siberian region, which may contain large quantities of oil reserves but is located in a far-flung area with little existing infrastructure, where construction and drilling are difficult during the winter months.

- *Natural depletion:* Efforts have been made to prolong the life of existing fields in Southeast Asia through the use of steam injection, but success has been limited, the EIA has reported. Following the project at the Duri field on Sumatra, for example, production actually dropped by roughly 0.071 mmbpd in 2003 (half of the drop was attributed to natural depletion).

- *Indonesia's declining production:* The production level and capacity of Indonesia are declining due to natural depletion. The country's oil infrastructure lacks necessary investment in its exploration and downstream sector. The EIA estimates that Indonesia's production capacity in 2001 and 2025 will be the same, 1.5 mmbpd. There are, however, some signs of improvement in investment. As noted above, the new Cepu oil field, estimated to hold reserves of at least 600 million barrels of oil, is being developed by ExxonMobil in partnership with Pertamina. Alleged corruption charges against Pertamina and continued disagreements over profit sharing and technical assistance beyond 2020 continue to stunt the development of Cepu.

- *Chinese exploration:* Most Chinese oil production capacity, close to 90 percent, is located onshore. One field alone, Daqing in northeastern China, accounts for about 1.0 mmbpd of China's production, out of total crude oil production of about 3.4 mmbpd. Daqing, however, is a mature field. Production began in 1963. Its production fell by 3.5 percent in 2003. At China's second-largest producing field, Liaohe in the northeast, the China National Petroleum Corporation has contracted with several foreign firms for work to enhance oil recovery and extend the life of the field.

- *Chinese refining bottlenecks:* In the late 1990s, as many as 110 small refineries were shut down. Now key Chinese oil companies are trying to upgrade existing refineries: (1) The China National Off-shore Oil Corporation has a 0.240-mmbpd refinery project in the city of Huizhou in Guangdong province, which is expected to become operational in early 2008. (2) ExxonMobil and Saudi Aramco signed a contract to expand the refining capacity of the Quongang refinery in Fujian from 0.080 to 0.24 mmbpd. (3) The China National Petroleum Corporation is planning a major expansion of the Dushanzi refinery in Xinjiang, which will be partially supplied by the new pipeline from Kazakhstan.

■ *Lagging energy sector in Australia:* Australia's oil fields have matured, and they need to be upgraded with new technologies in addition to expanding the exploration program, but the government has made cuts to exploration costs. Australian tax laws have been seen as obstacles to large foreign investment. In addition to declining production and discovery rates, Australia has eight refineries, and all of them have had declining gross margins for several years, mainly due to competition from foreign refineries benefiting from economies of scale.

EUROPE AND EURASIA

The Europe-Eurasia region covers all of Europe including the North Sea, Western Europe, Eastern Europe, FSU states, and the Caspian Sea area. As figure 5.9 shows, the two subregions that are rich in petroleum resources are the Caspian Sea area and the North Sea. In 2004, Europe and Eurasia had a total of 139.2 billion barrels of proven reserves. Since 1993, there has been a growth of 20 billion barrels of oil.

National Developments

The country with the largest oil reserves is Russia, with 225.95 billion barrels of known reserves, only 72.3 billion barrels of them proven. In addition, according to the *USGS 2000*, Russia has the second largest undiscovered oil reserves after Saudi Arabia, 77.38 billion barrels. The EIA does not report Russia's production capacity, but figure 5.10 shows that the total FSU oil production capacity in 2002 was 11.2 mmbpd and is projected to reach 17.6 mmbpd for the reference case in 2025.

Figure 5.9
Europe-Eurasia Proven, Known, Undiscovered Oil Reserves
(billion barrels)

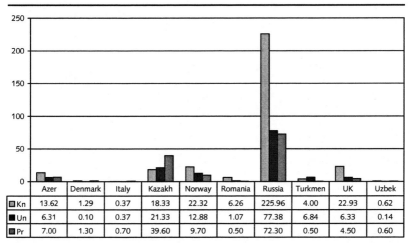

	Azer	Denmark	Italy	Kazakh	Norway	Romania	Russia	Turkmen	UK	Uzbek
Kn	13.62	1.29	0.37	18.33	22.32	6.26	225.96	4.00	22.93	0.62
Un	6.31	0.10	0.37	21.33	12.88	1.07	77.38	6.84	6.33	0.14
Pr	7.00	1.30	0.70	39.60	9.70	0.50	72.30	0.50	4.50	0.60

Source: Adapted by the authors from BP, *Statistical Review of World Energy 2005*, and
    the *U.S. Geological Survey 2000*.
Note: Azer = Azerbaijan; Kazakh = Kazakhstan; Turkmen = Turkmenistan;
    Uzbek = Uzbekistan. Kn = known; Un = undiscovered; Pr = proven.

The Kremlin continues to advance the state's influence in the energy sector. Moreover, Russian oil companies, such as Yukos, have been accused of corruption and tax evasion. Due to uncertainty and instability, the inflow of investment in the Russian oil sector has slowed down. In late September 2005, the Moscow City Court upheld the conviction of Mikhail Khodorkovsky, the former head of Yukos, who is accused of tax evasion. Khodorkovsky has been in jail since October 2003, and he accuses Vladimir Putin's government of arresting him to break up Yukos Oil and increase its control over the Russian oil industry.[65]

On September 27, 2005, Gazprom, the state-controlled Russian energy company, announced that it would acquire 72.66 percent of Sibneft's shares for $13.01 billion. This sale will be financed by $12 billion from a consortium of Western banks. Alexei Miller, Gazprom's chief executive, was quoted as saying that "the businesses of Gazprom and Sibneft have a defined synergy. This will make Gazprom more effective both in Russia and the world oil and gas market."

Figure 5.10
U.S. EIA Estimates of Europe-Eurasia Oil Production Capacity
(million barrels per day)

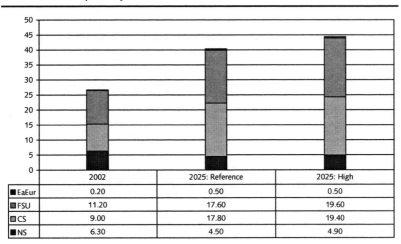

	2002	2025: Reference	2025: High
■ EaEur	0.20	0.50	0.50
▨ FSU	11.20	17.60	19.60
▨ CS	9.00	17.80	19.40
■ NS	6.30	4.50	4.90

Source: Adapted by the authors from U.S. Energy Information Administration,
International Energy Outlook 2005.
Note: EaEur = Eastern Europe; FSU = Former Soviet Union; CS = Caspian Sea;
NS = North Sea.

Many experts disagree. They see this as another attempt by the Kremlin to tighten its grip over the Russian oil sector, especially given the fact that Gazprom is buying the shares held by Roman Abramovich, a Russian billionaire with close ties to the Kremlin, who would gain $13 billion from the sale. In addition, they argue that the sale price is too low because the $13 billion works out to be $3.30 per barrel of reserves, which is lower than other recent oil deals.[66]

Russia does not allow foreigners to buy shares of Gazprom that are traded on the Russian market. It has announced, however, that it may relax some of these restrictions in the near future. Recently, Gazprom extracted about 545 billion cubic meters of gas per year and 1.17 mmbpd of crude oil.[67] However, it remains uncertain how the new purchase or future policy may influence it level of production.

Other FSU states such as Kazakhstan have seen significant foreign investment in their oil industry, but political instability and corruption continue to plague their energy sectors. Kazakhstan has the second largest reserves in the FSU after Russia. It has 18.327 billion barrels of known reserves and 39.6 billion barrels of proven reserves. According to the *USGS 2000*, it also has 21.327 billion barrels of undiscovered reserves, roughly more than twice its proven reserves.

Figure 5.10 shows that the Caspian Sea area has the potential to become a major oil and natural gas exporter during the next decade. The area is thought to hold the world's second largest oil and natural gas reserves after the Middle East. However, according to the EIA, several factors threaten to complicate the area's potential, including a lack of adequate export infrastructure, disagreement over new export routes, and border disputes between the littoral states.

The North Sea has the second largest reserves in the region. Figure 5.9 shows the oil reserves in the region. Norway and the United Kingdom hold the majority of the North Sea's reserves, with 9.7 billion barrels and 4.50 billion barrels of proven reserves, respectively. Denmark, the Netherlands, and Germany have smaller North Sea oil and natural gas resources.

According to the EIA, the region is a relatively high-cost producer because of the cold weather and the fact that it requires sophisticated offshore technology, but its political stability and proximity to major European consumer markets have allowed it to play a major role in world oil and natural gas markets. In fact, North Sea Brent oil is used as a benchmark. Brent oil is traded on the International Petroleum Exchange, and market forces reflect the price of Brent.[68]

Most of the North Sea countries have experienced slowing oil production growth in the past few years. The growth of the United Kingdom's and Norway's crude oil production has essentially come to a halt, and figure 5.10 shows that their production rates are projected to begin a long-term decline from a production capacity of 6.3 mmbpd in 2002 to between 4.3 and 4.9 mmbpd in 2025. In fact, only Germany has seen year-to-year growth in production. The fact that the output of Brent oil is too small has moved some analysts to question if Brent oil should continue to be used as a benchmark. The new Platts system therefore has widened its definition of Brent oil to include other North Sea oil in calculating the price.[69]

Key Strategic Challenges

Russia and the other FSU states present different challenges from Western European states. Russia faces long-term problems of a lack of transparency, the vulnerability of its oil facilities, and higher water cut rates. The Caspian Sea states lack the level of investment needed to upgrade their oil infrastructure and increase their recovery and discovery rates. Conversely, the North Sea faces the problems of aging fields that may have started their long-term decline.

The key security and socioeconomic challenges faced by the countries in Europe and Eurasia include:

- *Loose nuclear devices:* Before its collapse in 1991, the Soviet Union had about 27,000 nuclear weapons. Experts argue that these devices are dispersed around the FSU countries and are poorly guarded. Moreover, former FSU nuclear scientists, due to poverty and a lack of job opportunities, could be lured to help rogue states or terrorist organizations acquire nuclear weapons.

- *Political instabilities in the FSU:* In recent years, "revolutions" took place in FSU states such as Georgia, Ukraine, and Uzbekistan. Though most of these movements were peaceful forces for change, such was not the case in Uzbekistan. These instabilities add to uncertainty and prolong economic development.

- *Russia's reemergence:* Under Putin, Russia has tried to expand its influence over former satellite states in Eastern Europe and Central Asia. Though it is harder to know Russia's intentions, it is clear that recent Russian involvement in the internal affairs of FSU countries has been a destabilizing force. Moreover, Chechnya's quest for independence continues to preoccupy Russia due to bombings of both soft and military targets in Russia.

- *Sleeper cells in Western Europe:* Investigation of the 9/11 attacks and the Madrid bombing has shown that significant Al Qaeda cells exist. Law enforcement initiatives in the United Kingdom, Germany, and Spain have succeeded in breaking up some of these cells. Experts, however, believe that major cells still function in many Western European countries.

- *Immigration:* Recent events in the Netherlands and France have shown the tensions that exist between immigrants and many Europeans. Due to aging populations, many European economies need cheap labor. The tension is unlikely to go away as long as there is a lack of assimilation of immigrants into the general population.

Production Risks and Developments

The oil production of the Caspian Sea states has increased by roughly 70 percent since they gained independence from the Soviet Union. Most of the increase has come from the northern Caspian countries Kazakhstan and Azerbaijan. Other countries in the region have seen less substantial progress toward developing their energy industry since 1992. Large multinational oil companies have tried to win oil projects in Azerbaijan, Kazakhstan, Turkmenistan, and Uzbekistan, but they have not been able to land any major deals from the governments.[70]

According to the EIA, both onshore and offshore North Sea oil production totaled 5.9 mmbpd in 2005, approximately 5.6 percent less than in 1999. In 2005, Norway's production accounted for 57 percent and the United Kingdom accounted for 30 percent of the total North Sea output, making them the largest producers in the North Sea. These two nations, however, continue to experience a year-to-year decline in their production.[71]

The Caspian and North Seas regions must deal with the following developments and challenges:

- *Caspian Sea projects:* The Caspian Sea states have seen an increase in their production and proven reserves. In 2004, projects like Tengiz and Karachaganak (in Kazakhstan), and Azerbaijan's Azeri, Chirag, and deepwater Gunashli (ACG) field produced roughly 0.644 mmbpd—and these projects are expected to increase production to 1.7 mmbpd by 2010.

- *Russian oil turmoil:* Analysts blame the turmoil in the Russian oil industry on privatization of the industry and the subsequent corruption of oil tycoons. However, the privatization drive is also seen as a reason to improve incentives and increase the use of new technologies to upgrade mature oil infrastructure, which in turn will increase production at lower costs. Overall, Russia's production has increased. Siberian oil fields were increasing at 14 percent a year starting in the early 1990s. However, since the "nationalization" of the main production branch of the Yukos oil company, Yuganskneftegas, in December 2004, the flow of oil from the richest Siberian oil fields has stopped. In 2005, it was projected to produce the same amount of oil as in 2004, 385 million barrels.[72]

- *Kremlin control over the energy sector:* Many analysts believe that the drop in the Siberian oil fields' production is due to Russia's mismanagement of the nationalization process. The state-controlled company Rosneft took over from Yuganskneftegas after it was nationalized. The takeover of the company was part of the payment for a $28 billion tax claim against Yukos. In addition, the Kremlin is also seen as attempting to buy out Russia's fifth largest oil company, Sibneft, which produced 0.900 mmbpd. If this deal goes through, the Kremlin will increase its holdings to one-quarter of all Russian production.[73]

- *Instability in Kazakhstan:* Kazakhstan has seen many flows of foreign capital into its oil industry. Its oil production capacity has increased in recent years, but the growth rate could have been higher. The lack of political and economic stability has prevented these investments from producing the results they otherwise would have, given the potential of the oil industry. Other experts, however, attribute the decrease in the growth rates to restrictive government policies.

- *Barents Sea exploration resumption:* There have been two discoveries in the Norwegian part of the North Sea. According to the EIA, Statoil discovered oil at its Linerle prospect and delimited its Alve discovery well. In addition, it was reported that oil companies planned to start drilling for oil in the Barents Sea, marking the end of the suspension that started in 2001 in order to study the environmental impact of explorations.

- *The UK's maturing oil fields:* The EIA reported that the UK oil industry has shifted its focus from exploration to improving productivity and prolonging hydrocarbon extraction from its large, mature oil fields and developing smaller fields through the use of new technologies. High oil prices have provided the incentives for companies to invest in oil fields that were not considered "commercially viable."

- *Norway's maturing oil fields:* Although the North Sea will continue to be an important oil producer, its oil production from both the United Kingdom and Norway is on the decline. With new EOR technologies and large inflows of investment in their oil infrastructure, the life of their oil fields may be prolonged. There has been little in the area of new discovery, but Norway has attempted to focus on increasing the recovery rates of existing oil fields.

NORTH AMERICA

North America's oil reserves, which are shown in figure 5.11, have been declining since the 1980s. According to the BP *Statistical Review of World Energy 2005*, North America had 101.9 billion barrels of proven reserves in 1984. In 2004, its proven reserves had decreased to 61.0 billion barrels. Its oil production has also declined during the same period. It produced 14.150 mmbpd in 2004 compared with 13.807 mmbpd in 1994[74] and 14.838 mmbpd in 1983.[75]

National Developments

U.S. production capacity was 9.3 mmbpd in 2002. The EIA forecasts show that the United States' oil production capacity will increase only marginally or even plateau. In 2025, the United States will have a production capacity of 9.3 mmbpd for the reference case and 11.0 mmbpd for the high-price case, as shown in figure 5.12. The *Oil and Gas Journal* reported that the United States had 21.9 billion barrels of proven oil reserves as of January 1, 2005.[76]

The United States has more than 500,000 producing oil wells, but according to the Department of Energy, most of them are classified as "marginal" or "stripper" wells. This means that those wells have marginal production. For 2003, the major oil-producing areas included the Gulf of Mexico (1.6 mmbpd), Texas onshore (1.1), Alaska's North

Figure 5.11
North America Proven, Known, Undiscovered Oil Reserves
(billion barrels)

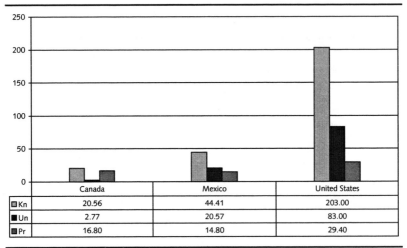

	Canada	Mexico	United States
Kn	20.56	44.41	203.00
Un	2.77	20.57	83.00
Pr	16.80	14.80	29.40

Source: Adapted by the authors from BP, *Statistical Review of World Energy 2005*, and
the *U.S. Geological Survey 2000*.
Note: Kn = known; Un = undiscovered; Pr = proven.

Figure 5.12
U.S. EIA Estimates of North America Oil Production Capacity
(million barrels per day)

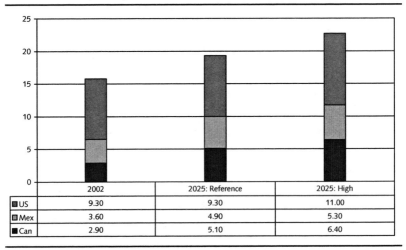

	2002	2025: Reference	2025: High
US	9.30	9.30	11.00
Mex	3.60	4.90	5.30
Can	2.90	5.10	6.40

Source: Adapted by the authors from U.S. Energy Information Administration,
International Energy Outlook 2005.
Note: US = United States; Mex = Mexico; Can = Canada.

Slope (0.949), California (0.683), Louisiana onshore (0.244), Oklahoma (0.178), and Wyoming (0.143).[77]

There has been much debate about the size of reserves in Alaska, and their expected production. Current technology and simulation models cannot predict exact reserves, cost of production, or the grade of oil in the Arctic National Wildlife Refuge (ANWR). At this point, all that is certain is that production in the ANWR also depends on the price of crude oil. The EIA has summarized its views on oil in the ANWR as follows:

> Alaskan crude oil production originates mainly from the North Slope, which includes the National Petroleum Reserve–Alaska (NPR–A) and the State lands surrounding Prudhoe Bay. Because oil and gas producers are prohibited from building permanent roads in NPR–A, exploration and production are expected to be about 30 percent more expensive than is typical for the North Slope of Alaska. Because drilling is currently prohibited in the Arctic National Wildlife Refuge (ANWR), AEO2005 does not project any production from ANWR; however, an EIA analysis [of 142] projects [states] that if drilling were allowed, production would start 10 years later and reach 900,000 barrels per day in 2025 if the area contains the mean level of resources (10.4 billion barrels) estimated by the U.S. Geological Survey.
>
> In the reference case, crude oil production from Alaska is expected to decline to about 810,000 barrels per day in 2010. After 2010, increased production from NPR–A raises Alaska's total production to about 890,000 barrels per day in 2014. Depletion of the oil resource base in the North Slope, NPR–A, and southern Alaska oil fields is expected to lead to a decline in the State's total production to about 610,000 barrels per day in 2025.
>
> As in the lower 48 States, oil production in Alaska is marginally sensitive to projected changes in oil prices. Higher prices make more of the reservoir oil-in-place profitable. In 2025, Alaska's production is projected to be about 100,000 barrels per day above the reference case level in the high A oil price case and 60,000 barrels per day below the reference case level in the low oil price case.[78]

The recent energy legislation passed in the U.S. Congress seems unlikely to accomplish anything that high oil prices would not accomplish without it. Critics are probably correct in stating that its main impact will be some $20 to $60 billion in needless aid and subsidies to various special interests.

Even high oil prices and market forces, however, are unlikely to halt the growth of U.S. import dependence through 2025. There are no meaningful near-term and midterm options that will allow the United States to reduce its dependence on foreign petroleum exports in any significant strategic sense. The United States must shape its security policies accordingly, regardless of what happens in Iraq.

Canada, conversely, claims that it has tapped into "new" sources of liquid fuel, including coal liquefaction, gas liquefaction, biomass, natural generation, oil shale, and tar sands. Moreover, it claims 179 billion barrels of tar sands, second only to Saudi Arabia.[79] In addition, in 2005, *Oil and Gas Journal* reported that Canadian oil reserves were 178.8 billion barrels, but more than 95 percent of the reserves are oil sand deposits in Alberta.[80]

Analysts predict that oil sand production will increase significantly in coming years and offset the decline in Canada's conventional crude oil production. Though the Canadian tar sands sound promising, extracting oil from them is costly and requires new technologies. Current production costs are $8 to $13 a barrel for bitumen and $18 to $23 a barrel for synthetic light oil. Currently, extraction from mining and upgrading produces 20 percent recovery, and steam-assisted gravity drainage and solvents are expected to produce 80 percent ultimate recovery.[81]

Canada has invested $28 billion since 1996, and it is now producing more than 1.0 mmbpd. It is expected to invest another $36 billion during the period 2005–2010. During the same period, production is expected to rise to 2.7 mmbpd.[82] Figure 5.12 shows that the EIA projects that Canada's production capacity can reach 5.1 mmbpd in 2025 for the reference case, and 6.4 mmbpd for the high-price case.

Mexico has the third largest proven reserves in North America. In 2004, it had 14.8 billion barrels of proven reserves. Figure 5.11 shows that according to the *USGS 2000*, Mexico had 44.41 billion barrels of known oil reserves and 20.570 billion barrels of undiscovered oil reserves.

There is some debate over the nature of Mexican oil reserves. In September 2002, Pemex, the national oil company, claimed that its estimates of proven crude had declined by 53 percent, to 12.6 billion barrels. Later it raised its proven reserve estimates to 15.7 billion barrels. In June 2004, Fernando Elizondo, Mexico's energy secretary, announced that Mexico had 18.9 billion barrels of proven reserves, which he claimed could run out in 11 years.[83]

Mexico's government budget relies heavily on oil revenues from Pemex. In 2003, these revenues represented 33 percent of the budget. Pemex pays roughly two-thirds of its oil revenues to the government, and 8 percent to cover pension liabilities. According to the EIA, these obligations—along with the fact that Pemex relies on the Congress for its budget—are making it more difficult to invest in expanding production capacity and explore for new discoveries.[84]

Figure 5.12 shows that Mexico's oil production capacity was 3.6 mmbpd in 2002. The EIA forecasts that the country's production capacity can reach up to 5.3 mmbpd in 2025 for the high-price case and 4.9 mmbpd for the reference case. This forecast, however, was based on lower prices and was made before the latest speculations by Mexico's secretary of energy that the country's oil reserves could run out in 11 years.

Key Strategic Challenges

Unlike other regions, countries in North America have not experienced the sabotage of their oil facilities or rebels demanding higher shares of oil revenues. There is little chance of a large-scale war in North America, although key facilities, population centers, and food supplies remain venerable to attacks by terrorists.

The following list summarizes the major long-term uncertainties that affect oil developments in the countries of North America:

- *Homeland security:* Following the 9/11 attacks, the U.S. administration created the Department of Homeland Security. However, the U.S. homeland continues to be vulnerable to attack. The U.S. borders with Mexico and Canada are not very well protected, and terrorist organizations may use them to infiltrate the country.

- *Immigration:* In light of the terrorist attacks, immigration is of national security importance to the United States. There are nearly 20 million illegal aliens. There is a need for a realistic and effective immigration policy that enforces current U.S. laws and deals with the economic needs of Mexico and other Central American countries. Canadian immigration and asylum laws have also been under scrutiny since the 9/11 attacks.

- *Poverty and instability in Mexico:* One cause of high immigration into the United States from Mexico is the lack of economic opportunities in Mexico.

- *Good governance in Mexico:* Though the political system in Mexico has become more stable, corruption—or at least the perception of it—continues to plague the system. This perception of corruption is an impediment to good governance.

- *Twin deficits:* The massive trade imbalance with China and the skyrocketing federal budget deficit are still sustainable, but they may exert pressure on future generations through higher taxes and a weaker dollar.

- *Aging populations and the entitlement programs:* The aging population in the United States and Canada will have economic and cultural implications in the long term. Programs such as Medicare and Social Security need more workers relative to retirees, but the demographic forces are limiting the ability of these programs to survive and support themselves. They are becoming too expensive for taxpayers.

Production Risks and Developments

Oil fields in the United States and Mexico are maturing. Some analysts have argued that they have started their long-term decline and claim that current reserve estimates are debatable.

As mentioned above, one estimate predicts that Mexico's reserves could run out in 11 years. Other experts claim that due to the lack of investment, Mexico's replacement rate is too low. They argue that with the right amount of capital investment in the oil industry—including enhanced recovery technology and intensive exploration—Mexico can improve its replacement rate and prolong the life of its current fields.

After years of debate, the U.S. Congress narrowly passed a bill to allow drilling on the coastal plain of the ANWR by inserting a provision for such drilling in the budget resolution for fiscal 2006; however, as of this writing, the bill has not yet been signed into law.

It is uncertain how much oil reserve the ANWR actually contains. The USGS 1998 estimates that the mean estimate of recoverable oil and natural gas liquids in the coastal ANWR is 10.3 billion barrels (with a 95 percent chance that 5.7 billion barrels of oil are recoverable and a 5 percent chance that 16 billion barrels are recoverable).[85] This could increase domestic oil production by a mean of 0.876 mmbpd at its peak in 2024. But access to ANWR oil would only lessen U.S. dependence on foreign oil by approximately 4 percent in the reference case, according to the EIA.[86]

There is more reason for optimism with regard to Canada's oil reserves. Most analysts believe that Canada has the potential to increase its production capacity. Canada faces slightly different problems. Though estimates differ, most agree that the Canadian tar sands contain 170 to 185 billion barrels of oil reserves. The issue is not whether these reserves exist, but rather the cost of extracting them and the availability of the right extraction technology.

The following major production uncertainties affect petroleum development in the United States, Canada, and Mexico:

- *The U.S. refining capacity and inventory buildup:* The United States' lack of ability to refine crude oil and distribute it to the domestic market in a timely manner can create bottlenecks that not only squeeze the average consumer but also negatively affect demand by driving up the price of crude futures because of a product-driven market. Gas ports, pipelines, and distribution system constraints have equal effects on gas supply.

- *Mexico's maturing oil fields:* Some experts believe that Pemex, the state-owned company, is unable to make any new discoveries and modernize existing infrastructure. The Vicente Fox administration has proposed opening the industry up to foreign investment to explore for offshore oil in the Gulf of Mexico.

■ *Cantarell upgrade:* Production from the largest oil field in Mexico, Cantarell, with an estimated 35 billion barrels of oil, witnessed a decline in the 1990s. Pemex inaugurated a project to use nitrogen injection to increase pressure and prolong the depletion, and the project was completed in 2001. By 2002, it showed remarkable recovery in that it doubled its 1995 production level. However, some have argued that Cantarell's decline could come as soon as mid-2005.

■ *Canadian oil sands:* The main issue with tar sand is the fact that most of the deposits contain heavy or "viscous" oil, which is harder to extract and costly to refine. According to the EIA, the problem is that the bitumen oil is too deep below the surface to use open pit mining. A method that is used is called in situ (in place), which uses steam to separate bitumen from the sand and push it to collection pools near the surface.

■ *U.S. Gulf of Mexico production:* Recently, the U.S. production from the Gulf of Mexico has increased due to more efficient deepwater wells, which account for about two-thirds of total U.S. Gulf output.

■ *Natural disasters:* As noted earlier, natural disasters in production, export, or refining areas can be damaging to the energy market. Hurricanes in the Gulf of Mexico have caused supply and distribution disruptions in the United States and have added large premiums to the price of a barrel of oil. In 2005, hurricanes Katrina and Rita shut down most of the refineries in the U.S. Gulf of Mexico, forcing the United States to release some of its strategic petroleum reserves, and they had a major impact on domestic gas production and prices and the need for imports.

■ *U.S. North Slope:* The Alaskan slopes contain the largest oil field in North America, Prudhoe Bay. In addition, according to the U.S. Department of Energy, as much as 36 billion barrels of original-

Figure 5.13
South and Central America Proven, Known, Undiscovered Oil Reserves (billion barrels)

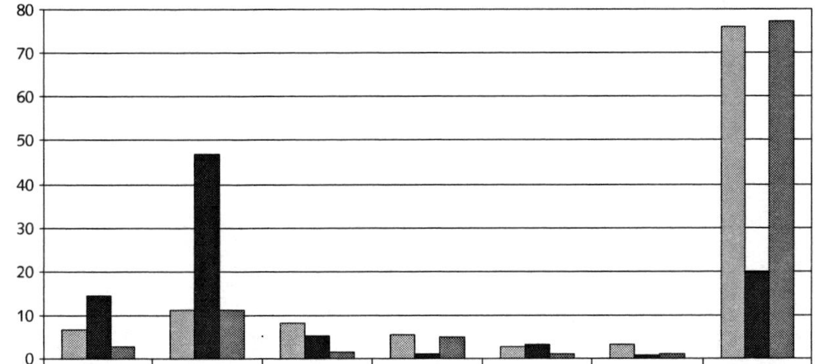

	Argentina	Brazil	Colombia	Ecuador	Peru	Trinidad	Venezuela
Kn	6.78	11.16	8.13	5.45	2.66	3.29	76.04
Un	14.52	46.75	5.12	0.97	3.32	0.76	19.66
Pr	2.70	11.20	1.50	5.10	0.90	1.00	77.20

Source: Adapted by the authors from BP, *Statistical Review of World Energy 2005*, and the *U.S. Geological Survey 2000*.
Note: Kn = known; Un = undiscovered; Pr = proven.

oil-in-place lay within the Ugnu, West Sak, and Schrader Bluff formations. The largest sources of potential oil are the heavy oil formations near the main producing zones at Prudhoe and Kuparuk.

SOUTH AND CENTRAL AMERICA

Figure 5.13 shows current estimates of Latin American oil reserves, and figure 5.14 shows current estimates of production capacity. South and Central American production totaled 5.17 mmbpd in 1983, and it increased to 6.764 mmbpd in 2004. Most of the production is led by Venezuela, the fourth largest oil exporter to the United States (behind Mexico, Saudi Arabia, and Canada). Venezuela exported 1.315 mmbpd of oil to the United States in March 2005. However, President Hugo Chávez has recently threatened to cut off all oil exports to the United States, claiming that the U.S. market is not vital to Venezuela's export market.[87]

Figure 5.14
U.S. EIA Estimates of South America Oil Production Capacity
(million barrels per day)

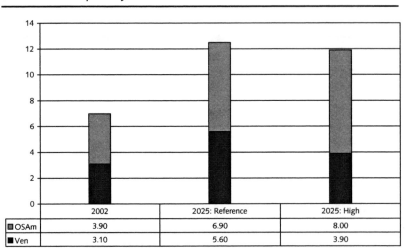

	2002	2025: Reference	2025: High
OSAm	3.90	6.90	8.00
Ven	3.10	5.60	3.90

Source: Adapted by the authors from U.S. Energy Information Administration, *International Energy Outlook 2005.*
Note: OSAm = Other South America; Ven = Venezuela

National Developments

On December 2, 2002, workers from Venezuela's state-owned oil company, Petroleos de Venezuela S.A. (PdVSA), joined the strike of the political opposition to President Chávez. The labor strike caused the total shutdown of parts of the oil industry and caused a large decline in Venezuela's oil production. This resulted in Chávez dismissing 50 percent of PdVSA's labor force.

The actual levels of oil production and production capacity in Venezuela before and after the 2002 strike are uncertain. Reports by international agencies, U.S. industry, and the Venezuelan government all differ in fundamental ways. The EIA summarized the uncertainty surrounding Venezuelan oil production capacity as follows:

Venezuela's actual level of crude oil production is difficult to determine, with the country and independent industry analysts offering different numbers. According to statements by the Venezuelan government, the country produced 3.1 million barrels per day (bbl/d) of crude oil in 2004. On the other hand, most industry analysts and EIA estimated that the country actually produced 2.5–2.6 million bbl/d of crude oil in 2004, as they believed the country had not fully recovered from the strikes of 2002–2003 and noted that [gross domestic product] data released by the Venezuelan Central Bank supported a lower level of production. Further, in a statement filed with the U.S. Securities and Exchange Commission (SEC) in August 2005, PdVSA reported that nationwide crude production in 2003 was 2.76 million bbl/d (PdVSA must file regular financial statements with the SEC due to its external debt obligations).

In the past, Venezuela regularly exceeded its OPEC production quota. However, since his election in 1998, President Chávez has maintained a policy of strong adherence to the country's quota, seeking to increase oil revenues through higher world oil prices rather than increased production. In order to meet its quota, Venezuela has occasionally shut-in some production and delayed bringing new capacity online. Most independent analysts believe, though, that Venezuela is currently producing well below its quota of 3.22 million bbl/d since the 2002–2003 strike.[88]

According the EIA reference-case forecast, Venezuela's oil production capacity is estimated to reach 3.9 to 5.6 mmbpd in 2025—as is shown in figure 5.14. Conversely, according to Venezuela's government, PdVSA plans to increase its production to 5.8 mmbpd by 2012 and 7.7 mmbpd by 2030. This expansion plan is estimated to cost $56 billion. These claims are not verifiable.

The rest of the region had a production capacity of 3.9 mmbpd. By 2025, its output could surpass Venezuela's. The EIA projects that other South and Central American countries' production capacity could reach 6.9 mmbpd for the reference case and 8.0 mmbpd for the high-price case.

Despite limited production, the South American continent has the third highest proven oil reserves in the world after the Middle East and Eurasia. Figure 5.13 shows that South and Central America had 101.2 billion barrels in 2004. Venezuela contains most of these reserves, with 77.2 billion barrels, the largest oil reserves outside the Middle East.

This number, however, does not include extra-heavy and bitumen deposits, which are estimated to total 235 to 270 billion barrels. The Chávez government has claimed that the Venezuelan government is increasing its investment and attracting foreign investment to develop its extra-heavy oil reserves.

Brazil has the second highest levels of proven oil reserves. Figure 5.13 shows that Brazil has 11.2 billion barrels of proven reserves and 46.746 billion barrels of undiscovered oil reserves. This total is followed by Venezuela, with 19.664 billion barrels; and Argentina, with 14.516 billion barrels. This discrepancy between oil reserves and production is due to the region's failure to take advantage of technological gains, ongoing political and security instabilities, and rigid laws that limit investment in the energy industry.

Brazil has the highest "undiscovered" oil reserves in the region and the fifth largest in the world. At the same time, it is the tenth largest oil consumer in the world and the third largest in the Western Hemisphere, after the United States and Canada. According the EIA, Brazil has made great strides in increasing its total oil production.[89] By 2004, Brazil's domestic production nearly met domestic demand. It produced an average of 1.542 mmbpd, and it hopes that by 2010, its production capacity can reach 2.3 mmbpd. To achieve this goal, Brazil has started a reform process for its oil industry.

Brazil is trying to partially privatize its energy sector and allow foreign companies to participate in developing its infrastructure. The EIA has reported, however, that

> despite these encouraging developments, Brazil's energy sector is still hampered by problems. Energy privatization has stalled, and Petrobras' presence in the oil and natural gas sectors remains pervasive, possibly slowing the development of competitive markets and the attraction of foreign investment. In addition, Brazil is still recovering from the 2001 energy crisis, which forced the government to implement a power-rationing program. The crisis highlighted Brazil's dependence on hydropower and its need to diversify the country's fuel mix. Since then, the da Silva administration has introduced new legislation for electricity and natural gas that would

help avert a future energy crisis, but it remains unclear whether the new regulations will guarantee supply. Analysts are also skeptical about Brazil's attempt to become oil self-sufficient, questioning how long the country would be able to maintain this status once reached, particularly with a burgeoning population and a recovering economy. With oil consumption likely to increase significantly in coming years, the question remains whether increased domestic oil output will simply offset domestic demand.[90]

Argentina is another major oil producer in Latin America. The EIA reports that it has 2.9 billion barrels of proven oil reserves, while BP claimed that Argentina contains 2.7 billion barrels of proven reserves.[91] The EIA does not report current production capacity for Argentina, but it has reported that its production peaked in 1998 at 0.916 mmbpd and that its production has been declining since. In 2004, however, Argentina's production averaged 0.756 mmbpd, compared with its 0.393 mmbpd of oil consumption, which made it a net exporter of 0.363 mmbpd.[92]

Key Strategic Challenges

Latin America is important to the oil market for two key reasons. First, proximity to the United States, the world's largest oil consumer, and high U.S. dependence on foreign sources of energy make Latin America an attractive source. Second, the region is rich with natural resources, and supply disruptions from the region can have devastating influence on the world oil market and the overall health of the global economy.

According to the EIA, Venezuela has the largest oil reserves outside the Middle East. Regional and energy experts believe that recent events in the Latin American countries have shown the importance of the region to the world economy.

Latin American countries do, however, face three types of instability: political, economic, and security. As mentioned above, the resulting uncertainty has had a major impact on the production capacity of the region's three major countries, Argentina, Brazil, and Venezuela. The region's countries face the following particular uncertainties and risks:

- *Narcotics trafficking:* Illegal drugs continue to plague the two continents. Rebel groups have been a destabilizing force in the region. The uncertainty accompanied by the lack of security has caused a decline in foreign investment in the energy industry.

- *Economic instability:* Argentina is recovering from the 2002 financial crises, but large sovereign debt, a tenuous-at-best fiscal situation, and a lack of transparency continue to be real problems throughout the region in the near future.

- *Instability in Venezuela:* The 2002 labor strikes, violent unrest in the streets, and the referendum on the Chávez presidency have caused massive uncertainty regarding the future stability of the country. Many experts believe that the problem is not political instability per se but, rather, the Chávez government's relationship with the United States. Those experts argue that in the short term, the Chávez government is politically stable. It remains uncertain how recent high oil prices and oil revenues will influence the domestic political system, and vice versa.

- *The Venezuelan government's relations with the private sector:* The Chávez government has a fragile relationship with the private sector, which has led to mistrust between the private and public sectors. Venezuela's most successful companies are those owned by the state, such as PdVSA. It remains to be seen how recent high oil prices and high rates of economic growth will influence the growth of the private sector and its relations with the government.

- *Venezuela and Cuba:* Chávez's relations with Fidel Castro continue to worry the United States and may prevent any real inflow of U.S. investment to upgrade Venezuela's aging oil infrastructure. This is exacerbated by Chávez's threats to terminate oil exports to the United States as a rebuke for U.S. "aggressive" behavior toward his regime.

- *Weak domestic institutions and laws:* Countries such as Colombia and Peru suffer from weak judicial institutions. This has added to the uncertain nature of doing business in South America.

- *Political and economic uncertainty in other Andean states:* Venezuela is not the only country facing such uncertainties. Peru, Bolivia, and Ecuador continue to be clouded by weak political institutions. Trust levels with regard to the political systems and current governments are at an all-time low. Experts argue that economic and political fluctuations have become the norm in the Andean states, and this has contributed to the lack of inflows of foreign investment and the slow rates of modernizing their energy infrastructures.

- *Insurgency and terrorism:* Though terrorist activities in the region have been mainly directed against domestic targets, transnational terrorist organizations could find safe havens in Latin America due to its proximity to the United States and the ability to use illicit drug trafficking to finance their operations.

Production Risks and Developments

In addition to the strategic challenges outlined above, Latin American countries have had production setbacks. Some countries like Brazil have made strides in overcoming these challenges, but others such as Venezuela continue to suffer from them.

The region suffers from a lack of capital investment in its upstream, downstream, and exploration industries. This is due to many reasons, including the security and political instability in the region, but it is not limited to them. Latin America continues to suffer from rigid foreign investment and tax laws, powerful but inefficient national oil companies, and official government corruption.

The following key developments affect the oil industries of the Latin American countries:

- *Political strikes in Venezuela's production level:* In 2002, half of PdVSA's workers went on a strike following a political strike by groups opposing the Chávez government. The government fired 50 percent of the state-owned oil company's workforce, and a dramatic drop in the country's oil production ensued. It is important, however, to note that this was not a labor dispute but a political struggle between Chávez and his rival.

- *Venezuela's production level:* As just noted, the 2002 strikes caused a drop of more than 2.0 mmbpd in the country's production. PdVSA claims that its production is back to the prestrike level, but others—including former PdVSA workers and many industry analysts—claim that its production level is considerably lower than in 2002. Though it has been reported that the company has made major strides in restoring its production and refining capacity, the situation is too uncertain to know PdVSA's oil production level.

- *Lack of foreign investment:* Strikes, economic stagnation, oil concession laws, and political risks in South America have discouraged foreign investment in its upstream and downstream oil sector. This lack of investment has limited the ability of countries to expand their production capacity, take advantage of new technological improvements, improve exploration and recovery rates, and adapt new training techniques.

- *Rigid regulations in the energy industry:* The Chávez administration changed the Hydrocarbon Law to increase royalties paid by private companies to 20 to 30 percent from the previous 1 to 16.66 percent and granted PdVSA at least a 51 percent stake in any project regarding exploration, production, transportation, or initial storage of oil.

- *State-imposed price controls:* Due to the high oil prices in 2004, countries in South America, namely Argentina, imposed a price ceiling, causing a surge in demand and imposing pressure on limited domestic supply.

- *Argentina's production capacity:* Argentinean oil production is still recovering from the energy crisis of 2004; and, as mentioned above, this was compounded by government-imposed price controls. Argentina's oil production peaked in 1998 at 0.916 mmbpd; and, by 2004; its production level reached 0.692 mmbpd. Despite this, Argentina remains the third largest oil producer in Latin America, exporting 0.295 mmbpd in 2004.

- *Offshore exploration in Argentina:* According to the EIA, "two onshore basins produce 82 percent of Argentina's oil: Neuquen, in western-central Argentina; and Golfo San Jorge, in the southeast. In 2004, Petrobras Energia acquired a license to explore the CAA-1 and CAA-8 blocks located off the country's central-east coast. Nearly every oil company active in Argentina has plans to develop offshore fields, both in the central-east and Tierra del Fuego regions. These areas should also be a major center of exploration for the new, state-owned energy company, Enarsa, which will have control over all offshore concessions not already licensed to private companies."[93]

- *Colombia's declining oil production:* Colombia's oil production decreased by 5 percent from 2003 to 2004; and between 2004 to 2005, its proven reserves declined by 13 percent. This translates into a 58 percent reduction in exports to the United States.[94] This decline is mostly attributed to natural depletion of the Cusiana, Cupiagua, and Caño Limon oil fields (the largest of the three).

- *The security of oil facilities in Colombia:* Guerrilla groups have sabotaged pipelines and oil facilities in Colombia. These two developments—in addition to the lack of any new discoveries, according to the president of Colombia—may force Colombia to become an oil importer.

- *Exploration in Brazil:* There have been some discoveries in Brazil; but according to the IEA, many of them are viscous oil. In addition, most of them have been offshore and in deep water. These "geological disappointments" make production in Brazil an expensive undertaking and make foreign investment less attractive, which can further complicate Brazil's oil sector.

Notes

[1] U.S. Energy Information Administration (EIA), *World Energy Outlook 2004*, October 2004, 29.

[2] For more details on Saudi Arabia's efforts to secure its oil infrastructure, see Anthony Cordesman and Nawaf Obaid, "Saudi Petroleum Security: Challenges and Response," Center for Strategic and International Studies, November 30, 2005, available at http://www.csis.org/burke/saudi21/saudi _PetroleumSecurity041129.pdf.

[3] Christopher Dickey, "Saudi Storms," *Newsweek*, October 3, 2005, available at http://www.msnbc.msn.com/id/9468701/site/newsweek/.

[4] Jimmy Burns and Thomas Catan, "Oil Groups Face Rise in Threats to Security," *Financial Times*, October 4, 2005.

[5] Rick Jervis, "Iraq Oil Output Falls Behind the Pre-War Levels," *USA Today*, October 11, 2005.

[6] See http://www.eia.doe.gov/emeu/security/choke.html#HORMUZ. The strait is the narrow passage between Iran and Oman that connects the Persian Gulf with the Gulf of Oman and the Arabian Sea. It consists of 2-mile-wide channels for inbound and outbound tanker traffic, as well as a 2-mile-wide buffer zone. The EIA estimates that some 13.0 mmbpd flowed through the strait in 2002. The IEA puts the figure at 15 mmbpd in 2003. Both agencies indicate that the amount of oil moving by tanker will increase steadily as Asian demand consumes a larger and larger share of total exports.

Closure of the Strait of Hormuz would require the use of longer alternate routes (if available) at increased transportation costs. Such routes include the 5-mmbpd-capacity Petroline (East–West Pipeline) and the 290,000-bpd Abqaiq–Yanbu natural gas liquids line across Saudi Arabia to the Red Sea. Theoretically, the 1.65-mmbpd Iraqi Pipeline across Saudi Arabia (IPSA) also could be utilized, more oil could be pumped north to Ceyhan (Turkey), and the 0.5-mmbpd Tapline to Lebanon could be reactivated.

[7] IEA, *World Energy Outlook 2004*, tables 3.7–3.8.

[8] Ibid., 32.

[9] EIA, "World Crude Oil Production (Including Lease Condensate), 1997–Present," July 2005, available at http://www.eia.doe.gov/emeu/ipsr/t11a.xls.

[10] "Extra Funds Seen Needed for Iraq Reconstruction," Reuters, September 7, 2005, available at http://www.alertnet.org/thenews/newsdesk/N07207597.htm.

[11] "Iraq Pipeline Watch," IAGS Energy Security, September 9, 2005, available at http://www.iags.org/iraqpipelinewatch.htm.

[12] Christian T. Miller, "Missteps Hamper Iraqi Oil Recovery," *Los Angeles Times*, September 26, 2005.

[13] Alison Smale, "Iraq May Be Years from Returning to Peak Oil Output, Ex-Minister Says," *International Herald Tribune*, September 22, 2005, available at http://www.iht.com/articles/2005/09/21/business/oil.php.

[14] Jervis, "Iraq Oil Output Falls Behind the Pre-War Levels."

[15] EIA, "World Crude Oil Production (Including Least Condensate), 1997–Present."

[16] EIA, Country Analysis Brief, "Iran," March 2005, available at http://www.eia.doe.gov/emeu/cabs/iran.html.

[17] Ruba Husari, "New Tensions Flair on Iraq–Kuwait Border," *International Oil Daily*, August 8, 2005.

[18] EIA, Country Analysis Brief, "Kuwait," June 2005, available at http://www.eia.doe.gov/emeu/cabs/kuwait.html.

[19] "Gulf-Creeping Fundamentalism in Kuwait," *Jane's Islamic Affair Analyst*, November 26, 2004.

[20] EIA, Country Analysis Brief, "Oman," January 2005, available at http://www.eia.doe.gov/emeu/cabs/oman.html.

[21] EIA, Country Brief Analysis, "Qatar," February 2005, available at http://www.eia.doe.gov/cabs/qatar.html.

[22] Ibid.

[23] Sam Ghattas and Amy Teibel, "Qatar Offers Rare Praise for Israel," Associated Press, September 15, 2005, available at http://news.yahoo.com/news?tmpl=story&u=/ap/20050915/ap_on_re_mi_ea/un_summit_arabs_israel.

[24] EIA, Country Analysis Brief, "Saudi Arabia," August 2005, available at http://www.eia.doe.gov/emeu/cabs/saudi.html.

[25] "Saudi Production Hike Narrows Spare Capacity Cushion," Reuters, April 21, 2005.

[26] Richard W. Stevenson, "Bush and Saudi Prince Discuss High Oil Prices in Ranch Meeting," *New York Times*, April 26, 2005.

[27] EIA, Country Analysis Brief, "Saudi Arabia."

[28] Dickey, "Saudi Storms."

[29] Kim Murphy, "Oil Industry Is an Obvious Terrorist Target, Say Experts," *Daily Times*, April 19, 2005, available at http://www.dailytimes.com.pk/default.asp?page=story_19-4-2003_pg4_22.

[30] *OPEC Bulletin*, November/December 2004, 21–22.

[31] "Measured Growth," *Foreign Reports Bulletin*, March 22, 2005.

[32] *OPEC Bulletin*, November/December 2004, 21–22.

[33] "Saudi ARAMCO Awards $8 Billion Projects," UPI, March 17, 2005.

[34] EIA, Country Brief Analysis, "UAE," April 2005, available at http://www.eia.doe.gov/emeu/cabs/uae.html.

[35] "Abu Dhabi Kick Starts Expansion Race," *Upstream*, March 26, 2005, available at http://www.zawya.com/story.cfm/sidZAWYA20050326060246.

[36] Trade Arabia, "Abu Dhabi's IPIC Eyes Asia Downstream Expansion," August 23, 2005, available at http://www.tradearabia.com/tanews/newsdetails _snOGN_article92071_cnt.html.

[37] Simon Henderson, *UAE after Sheikh Zayed: Tension between Tribe and State*, Policy Watch 915 (Washington, D.C.: Washington Institute for Near East Policy, 2004).

[38] Simon Henderson, *Succession Politics in the Conservative Arab Gulf States: The Weekend's Events in Ras Al-Khaimah*, Policy Watch 769 (Washington, D.C.: Washington Institute for Near East Policy, July 2003).

[39] EIA, Country Brief Analysis, "Eastern Mediterranean Region," August 2005, available at http://www.eia.doe.gov/cabs/eastmed.html.

[40] "Egypt Signs Deal to Supply Gas to Neighbor Israel," *Upstream*, September 22, 2005.

[41] Catherine Hunter, "BG Offers Creative Solutions for Sale of Palestinian Gas to Israel," World Markets Research Centre, May 12, 2004.

[42] Paula Dittrick, "Israel Oil, Gas Targets Spark a Flurry of Drilling," *Oil and Gas Journal*, October 3, 2005.

[43] Catherine Hunter, "Israeli Prime Minister Performs Volte-Face over Gazan Gas Supplies," World Markets Research Centre, September 27, 2005.

[44] Gal Luft, "Africa Drowns in a Pool of Oil," *Los Angeles Times*, July 1, 2003.

[45] Cyril Widdershoven, "West African Oil: Hope of Hype," Institute for the Analysis of Global Security, July 16, 2003.

[46] Todd Pitman, "U.S. Strategic Interests Rise in West Africa's Oil-Rich Gulf of Guinea," Associated Press, August 7, 2005.

[47] Widdershoven, "West African Oil."

[48] Pitman, "U.S. Strategic Interests Rise in West Africa's Oil-Rich Gulf of Guinea."

[49] Craig Timberg, "Rebel Threat Disrupts Flow of Nigeria Oil," *Washington Post*, September 24, 2005, available at http://www.washingtonpost.com/wp-dyn/content/article/2005/09/23/AR2005092301878.html.

[50] Widdershoven, "West African Oil."

[51] Luft, "Africa Drowns in a Pool of Oil."

[52] Widdershoven, "West African Oil."

[53] Luft, "Africa Drowns in a Pool of Oil."

[54] EIA, Country Analysis Brief, "Sudan," available at http://www.eia.doe .gov/emeu/cabs/sudan.html.

[55] "Riots After Sudan VP Garag Dies," BBC News, available at http://news.bbc.co.uk/1/hi/world/africa/4734517.stm; EIA, "Sudan."

[56] EIA, Country Analysis Brief, "Sudan."

[57] John J. Fialka, "Search for Crude Comes with New Dangers," *Wall Street Journal*, April 11, 2005.

[58] Ibid.

[59] EIA, "Monthly Chronology," August 8, 2005, available at http://www.eia.doe.gov/emeu/cabs/MEC_Current/August.html.

[60] EIA, Country Analysis Brief, "Indonesia," available at http://www.eia.doe.gov/emeu/cabs/indonesia.html.

[61] EIA, Country Analysis Brief, "Japan," available at http://www.eia.doe.gov/emeu/cabs/japan.html.

[62] Ibid.

[63] EIA, Country Analysis Brief, "China," available at http://www.eia.doe.gov/emeu/cabs/china.html.

[64] Ibid.

[65] Peter Finn, "Russian Oil Tycoon's Conviction Upheld," *Washington Post*, September 23, 2005, available at http://www.washingtonpost.com/wp-dyn/content/article/2005/09/22/AR2005092201858.html.

[66] Peter Finn, "Russian Giant Expands Control of Oil," *Washington Post*, September 28, 2005.

[67] Garfield Reynolds, "Gazprom Agrees to Buy Sibneft Control for $13.1 Bln," Bloomberg News, September 28, 2005, available at http://quote.bloomberg.com/apps/news?pid=10000006&sid=aSk0e10qy6bM&refer=home#.

[68] EIA, Country Analysis Brief, "North Sea," available at http://www.eia.doe.gov/emeu/cabs/northsea.html.

[69] Ibid.

[70] EIA, Country Analysis Brief, "Caspian Sea," available at http://www.eia.doe.gov/emeu/cabs/caspian.html.

[71] EIA, Country Analysis Brief, "North Sea."

[72] Andrew Kramer, "The Slow Flow of Russian Oil," *New York Times*, September 20, 2005, available at http://www.nytimes.com/2005/09/20/business/worldbusiness/20stategaz.html.

[73] Ibid.

[74] BP, *Statistical Review of World Energy 2005*, June 2005.

[75] BP, *Statistical Review of World Energy 2005*, June 2004.

[76] EIA, Country Analysis Brief, "United States," available at http://www.eia.doe.gov/emeu/cabs/usa.html.

[77] Ibid.

[78] EIA, *Annual Energy Outlook 2005*, available at http://www.eia.doe.gov/oiaf/aeo/gas.html.

[79] Canadian Association of Petroleum Producers, National Energy Board.

[80] EIA, Country Analysis Brief, "Canada," available at http://www.eia.doe.gov/emeu/cabs/canada.html.

[81] Canadian Association of Petroleum Producers, National Energy Board.

[82] Ibid.

[83] EIA, Country Analysis Brief, "Mexico," available at http://www.eia.doe.gov/emeu/cabs/mexico.html.

[84] Ibid.

[85] EIA, "Potential Oil Production from the Coastal Plain of the Arctic National Wildlife Refuge: Updated Assessment," available at http://www.eia.doe.gov/pub/oil_gas/petroleum/analysis_publications/arctic_national_wildlife_refuge/html/execsummary.html.

[86] EIA, "Analysis of Oil and Gas Production in the Arctic National Wildlife Refuge," available at http://www.eia.doe.gov/oiaf/servicerpt/ogp/results.html.

[87] "Chávez Makes U.S. Oil Export Threat," BBC News, August 15, 2005, available at http://news.bbc.co.uk/2/hi/americas/4153318.stm.

[88] EIA, Country Analysis Brief, "Venezuela," available at http://www.eia.doe.gov/emeu/cabs/Venezuela/Oil.html.

[89] EIA, Country Analysis Brief, "Brazil," available at http://www.eia.doe.gov/emeu/cabs/brazil.html.

[90] Ibid.

[91] EIA, Country Analysis Brief, "Argentina," available at http://www.eia.doe.gov/emeu/cabs/argentina.html.

[92] BP, *Statistical Review of World Energy 2005*, June 2005.

[93] EIA, Country Analysis Brief, "Argentina."

[94] EIA, Country Analysis Brief, "Colombia," available at http://www.eia.doe.gov/emeu/cabs/Colombia/Background.html.

CHAPTER SIX

OIL PRODUCTION AND RECOVERY TECHNOLOGIES

Given finite resources, the natural depletion of oil fields is inevitable. To sustain the same level of production capacity, producers need to replenish the natural decline curve either through new discoveries or by enhancing recovery. Declining production from giant and supergiant oil fields has become increasingly hard to replace with new discoveries. However, technological gains have improved discovery and recovery rates.

Oil fields have three stages of development, which depend on the level of pressure in the oil field or reservoir that helps the flow of crude to the surface:[1]

- *Primary recovery:* During the first stage of extraction, production depends on the natural pressure of the reservoir. Sometimes wells are injected with fluids to improve or stimulate the natural pressure in the field.

- *Secondary recovery:* During the second stage of extraction, water or gas injections are used to increase the pressure in the field and to push materials up to the surface of the well.

- *Tertiary recovery:* During the third stage of extraction, gases such as carbon dioxide, and heat such steam or hot water, are used to increase the field's pressure.

Historically, the average recovery rate of an oil field has been about 30 percent. Some analysts, however, argue that the current recovery rates of some oil fields can be raised as high as 50 percent by increasing recovery efficiency.

Techniques developed to create enhanced oil recovery (EOR) methods have been applied to mature oil fields. EOR techniques refer to any recovery method other than the primary and conventional secondary recovery methods of "flooding" (with water or fire) or injecting steam or gas such as nitrogen or carbon dioxide. "All tertiary recovery methods are enhanced, but not all enhanced methods are tertiary."[2]

Diagnostic technologies such as three-dimensional seismic modeling have improved discovery rates as well as recovery efficiency by providing reservoir data to help in controlled directional drilling. There has been much debate about the nature of these technologies and the level of capital that has been invested in them. It is notable, however, that the nature of these technologies is as important as how they are used.

KEY TECHNOLOGICAL DEVELOPMENTS

The recent surge in demand for oil has put a strain on production capacity, and at this point, the world has little sustainable spare capacity. If oil producers are to ease the strain imposed by the lack of spare production capacity, they must improve their production rates by investing in finding new discoveries or improving recovery rates from existing fields.

During the past three decades, several kinds of technological breakthroughs have improved production and recovery rates. Oil companies around the world are developing these techniques or financing research and development (R&D) in this area. One area of focus is "integration" or reservoir technology, which analysts claim gives experts more data capabilities and improves their overall understanding of the fields. Recent technological developments and techniques include the following

- *Parallel oil, water, and gas reservoir simulator (POWERS):* This is part of the reservoir simulation process in the appraisal stage of the field management process. Because this is early in the process, oil companies do not have historical data to make any meaningful prediction. POWERS utilizes massive parallel processing technology to provide simulated data; using such data involves considerable uncertainty.

- *Maximum reservoir contact (MRC):* An MRC is a type of well that has long reservoir contact through a single or multilateral wellbore completion. Aramco claimed that initial assessments indicated that MRC wells could have a 30 percent reduction in cost.

- *Carbon dioxide (CO_2) EOR:* This has been increasingly used in the United States because of the large resources of CO_2. CO_2 EOR works by injecting CO_2 underground, and it "closes the carbon loop," which would have been lost in the atmosphere. The U.S. Department of Energy has been investing in CO_2 R&D since the 1970s, and it has been used in some projects in Kansas.[3]

- *Biocompetitive exclusion process:* This method replaces the traditional method of recovering tertiary oil. The benefits of this are that it significantly increases oil production with a lower cost than the traditional methods, it eliminates poisonous hydrogen sulfide in the production system, it improves secondary and tertiary recovery, and it enables the producer to recover large residual oil reserves.[4]

- *Real-time geosteering:* This technology enables asset teams to steer the direction of drilling a wellbore a mile or more underground. Satellite technology sends drilling and logging-while-drilling data directly from the drill bit to visualization centers, where experts analyze the data and navigate the wellbore trajectory through the reservoir.

- *Intelligent wells:* These enable experts to monitor a reservoir in real time to analyze the data and remotely initiate intervention if needed. Recent experience has increased the technology's reliability. At this point, the technology is expensive, but the technology offers accelerated production, improved recovery, and lower operational expense.

- *Horizontal wells:* It is debated how effective these wells are, but some have claimed that their productivity is several times that of offset vertical wells. The level of increase in productivity, however, depends on the characteristics of the reservoir. This gain is not without problems; logging such wells is challenging when a drill pipe has to go through the horizontal path of the well, which consumes time and is costly. However, effective use of these wells requires strong understanding of fracture type, fracture orientation, and facies distribution.[5]

- *Intelligent Downhole Network (IDN):* IDN is a new generation of pressure and temperature gauges, an advanced multipurpose Downhole Interface Module, and a subsea/topside Downhole Network. It offers communication, power, and interface for the completion of projects.[6]

- *Steam-assisted gravity drainage (SAGD):* SAGD, an in situ method, is the most promising thermal recovery technology for Canadian bitumen resources. SAGD employs horizontal wells drilled near the bottom of the reservoir, where the top horizontal well is used to inject steam and the bottom one collects the produced liquids. The injected steam from the upper well increases the formation and forms a large chamber of steam on top of the well. This steam then condenses and heats the oil, which allows it to drain into the production well. This drainage process leads to high oil rates and a high recovery rate for the original oil in place.[7]

THE IMPORTANCE OF INVESTING IN RESEARCH AND DEVELOPMENT

Key oil-exporting nations are reacting to the need to increase their use of advanced technology. Canada, for example, has announced that it is investing in developing new technologies to facilitate the production and recovery of Canadian tar sands. Saudi Arabia is also putting more money into R&D. The Saudi oil minister said on April 27, 2004, "Eventually, technological advances will usher in a new energy resource to replace oil. Oil will not cede its position as the pre-eminent fuel because the world runs dry, but because technology has rendered it less desirable. We in Saudi Arabia believe that there are sufficient quantities of oil left to make the transition to the next great energy source a smooth one."[8]

Notes

[1] Occidental Petroleum Corporation, "Enhanced Oil Recovery," available at http://www.oxy.com.

[2] Cogeneration Technologies, "Enhanced Oil Recovery," available at http://www.cogeneration.net/enhanced_oil_recovery.htm.

[3] National Energy Technology Laboratory, "CO_2 Injection Boosts Oil Recovery, Captures Emissions," January 10, 2005, available at http://www.sciencedaily.com/releases/2005/01/050110091718.htm.

[4] Lata Group, "New Technology for Sulfide Reduction and Enhanced Recovery," available at http://www.eere.energy.gov/inventions/pdfs/latagroupimpacts.pdf.

[5] Saudi Aramco, "Reservoir Management," 2002, 15.

[6] Ibid., 28.

[7] Ron Sawatzky, "In Situ Recovery Method for Heavy Oil and Bitumen," Alberta Research Council, Edmonton, Canada, CSEG National Convention, 2004.

[8] Speech by Oil Minister Ali Al-Naimi, "Minister Assures Oil Supply at Symposium in Washington, DC," April 27, 2005, available at http://saudiembassy.net/2004News/News/EneDetail.asp?cIndex=3444.

CHAPTER SEVEN

_____

CONCLUSION

DEALING WITH GLOBAL RISKS AND AN UNCERTAIN FUTURE

Many of the world's oil reserves exist in regions and countries that suffer from political, economic, social, and security instabilities. In the short term, there is little the world can do to change these uncertainties. Energy policies and planning, however, have to be geared more toward risk management than averting risks and toward improving understanding of the forces that shape the global energy market.

Reports by the U.S. Energy Information Administration and the International Energy Agency are considered by many in government, business, journalism, and academia as a key reference for energy reporting and analysis. They are also the most reliable picture of how governments see the future of world energy supply and demand. The annual *International Energy Outlook* of the EIA and the *World Energy Outlook* of the IEA have long been considered the best of these reports and key tools in analyzing energy policy.

The EIA published its annual *International Energy Outlook 2005* on July 29, 2005. This report has been issued at a time when oil prices are at an all-time high due to geopolitical and security risks, surges in the demand for oil, the U.S. refining capacity bottleneck, and the limited spare production capacity in some oil-producing nations.

The EIA's report does focus on a wide range of energy-related issues. It attempts to analyze world energy supply and demand in addition to outlining major developments in the world market for oil, natural gas, coal, and electricity. It also forecasts major indicators in the energy market, such as crude oil production capacity and world energy consumption by fuel.

However, it fails to fully come to grips with the most important single development in world energy supply. Last year's report by the EIA, the *IEO 2004*, was criticized by experts for not adjusting its forecasts for high oil prices, and it was considered out of date before it came out in April 2004.

The EIA did adjust its price forecast to take into account much higher oil prices, with a price range of $21 to $48 a barrel, and the introduction of the *IEO 2005* even indicates that the "high-price" case may be the most likely case. Unfortunately, however, even though it states that such high prices could radically reduce future oil consumption, the *IEO 2005* makes almost no meaningful analysis of the broader implications of such drastic shifts in the oil market and global energy balances. Its focus is almost solely on a reference case of $35 a barrel and different levels of global economic growth.

WHY HIGH PRICES CAN BE SO IMPORTANT

The price of oil is a major uncertainty that affects every aspect of global energy demand, production capacity, investment, and the elasticity of demand and supply. As mentioned above, the *IEO 2004* used unrealistically low prices. Analysts hoped that the *IEO 2005* would shed some light on the current energy market, taking into account high oil prices and realistic long-term effects of conservation and alternative sources of energy on the elasticity of demand. The *IEO 2004* projected that oil prices in 2025 will be $17 per barrel for the "low-price" case, $27 per barrel for the "reference" case, and $35 per barrel for the "high-price" case.

According to the *IEO 2005*, during 2004, oil prices rose by more than $9 a barrel. The *IEO 2005* forecasts are based on three cases for 2025: $21 per barrel for the low-price case, $35 per barrel for the reference case, and $48 per barrel for the high-price case. The report forecasts that oil prices will continue to rise in 2005, adding about $11 per barrel in 2005. The EIA report summarizes the following reasons for high oil prices:

First, world petroleum demand grew at a robust 3.4 percent (2.7 million barrels per day) in 2004, reflecting dramatic increases in China's demand for oil-generated power and oil-based transportation fuels, as well as a rebound in U.S. oil demand. Second, oil prices typically are sensitive to any incremental tightening of supply during periods of high economic growth. On the supply side, there was very little spare upstream capacity, and the spare downstream capacity was not always properly configured to produce the required slate of products. World oil inventories, in terms of "days of supply," were unusually low. Next, geopolitical tensions in major oil-producing countries—including the continuing war in Iraq and uncertain prospects for a return to normalcy in Iraq's oil sector—and potential unrest in Nigeria and Venezuela contributed to the volatility in world oil markets.[1]

The three scenarios presented in the *IEO 2005*'s forecasts use far more realistic price ranges than those used in the *IEO 2004*. As has been touched upon above, however, the reference case used in the EIA forecasts assumes that the price per barrel of oil will start declining and will reach $31 in 2010 and $35 in 2025. It never really addresses a high-price future, and the rationale for the steep decline in the future price of oil in the reference case is not clear.

Such a case is always possible, but it is anything but certain as a "reference." The *IEO 2005* should have used a parametric range of oil prices in a climate of much uncertainty. Economic forecasting always involves significant uncertainty, and history has shown that predicting oil prices is even more uncertain due to the many variables that can affect the oil market. In fact, even the introduction to the *IEO 2005* questions whether its "reference case" is the most probable case.

Using both the high-price case and the reference case seems to be the proper basis for more realistic forecasts than the low-price case. The low-price scenario can happen if a practical alternative to oil is reached, massive oil reserves are discovered, the world stops using oil, or oil-producing nations have no control over the short-term market.

Moreover, the definition of "world oil price" is misleading. The *IEO 2005* defines oil prices as the "imported refiners' acquisition cost"

(IRAC) of imported oil to the United States. According to the *IEO 2005*, on average, IRAC tends to be less than the cost of the higher-quality West Texas Intermediate crude. IRAC, however, provides a good benchmark as to what refiners are paying for crude oil and how much suppliers are getting. It also gives us a better idea of how the bottleneck in the U.S. refining capacity may have a direct influence on the "world price of oil."

OIL PRODUCTION AND PRODUCTION CAPACITY FORECASTS

These issues may seem technical and analytic quibbles, but they have massive policy implications. As table 7.1 shows, the high-price case of $48 in the *IEO 2005* analysis radically reduces the need for new oil production capacity and actual production, and it radically increases unconventional oil production from sources like Canadian tar sands and Venezuelan heavy crude—production that was not even analyzed in the *IEO 2004*.

There are problems in the EIA modeling approach that make it extremely difficult to estimate the credibility of such projections. The fact is that any assumptions about the impact of sustained high oil prices on petroleum supply, unconventional oil, the production of competing sources of energy like nuclear and coal, and conservation and efficiency are highly speculative. Moreover, few analysts and oil experts outside the EIA and IEA have ever believed that world oil production and production capacity could or would ever reach the levels projected in the low-price case for either the *IEO 2004* or *IEO 2005*, and many have doubted the credibility of the levels called for in the reference case.

Nevertheless, no one can disregard the potential importance of the *IEO 2005* high-price projections. They indicate that market forces would solve many supply problems if oil did reach the prices called for in this case, and that price rises produce a much steeper drop in demand than most analysts have previously thought would occur.

This illustrates a policy gap that was a critical problem in the *IEO 2004* projections, which only used comparatively low prices, and

Table 7.1
World Oil Production and Production Capacity in 2025: *IEO 2004* versus *IEO 2005* Projections (million barrels per day)

Region	2002 Actual	IEO 2004 Projections			IEO 2005 Projections		
		Low	Reference	High	Low	Reference	High
Price ($/barrel)	$23.78	$17.00	$27.00	$35.00	$21.00	$35.00	$48.00
Production capacity (mmbpd)							
PG	18.7	56.8	45.0	32.9	50.0	39.3	27.8
Al	1.3	3.0	2.7	2.2	3.7	2.8	2.2
Li	1.5	3.1	2.9	2.4	3.9	2.9	2.2
OME	1.4	2.6	2.8	3.1	2.7	2.8	3.0
OPEC	27.2	75.7	61.5	46.8	72.8	56.0	40.4
World total	69.4	137.0	126.1	117.3	135.2	122.2	115.5
PG as % **of total**	**26.95%**	**41.46%**	**35.69%**	**28.05%**	**36.98%**	**32.16%**	**24.07%**
Production (mmbpd)							
ME	19.0	29.9	42.1	54.0	48.4	36.9	25.7
OPEC	28.7	40.1	54.9	7.3	67.6	52.7	35.0
Uncon	0.0	6.5	4.7	3.9	4.3	5.7	10.5
Can	0.0	3.9	3.3	2.8	2.9	3.5	4.7
LAm	0.0	2.6	1.4	1.1	1.2	1.5	3.0
World total	78.1	112.7	12.6	132.5	130.9	118.9	112.9
PG as % **of total**	**24.30%**	**26.50%**	**34.80%**	**40.70%**	**37.00%**	**31.00%**	**18.40%**

Sources: Adapted by the authors from U.S. Energy Information Administration, *International Energy Outlook 2004*, and *International Energy Outlook 2005*.

Note: IEO totals include conventional and nonconventional oil. Nonconventional oil production is dominated by Canadian tar sands and Venezuelan heavy crude, which were not broken out as separate categories in the *IEO 2004* analysis. Total unconventional production is assumed to reach 5.7 million barrels per day (mmbpd) in the reference case by 2025. The figure is 10.5 mmbpd for the high-price case and 4.3 mmbpd for the low-price case. Total Middle Eastern unconventional oil production is only 0.1 mmbpd in the reference case, 0.6 mmbpd in the high-price case, and 0.0 mmbpd in the low-price case.

Note: PG = Persian Gulf; Al = Algeria; Li = Libya; OME = Other Middle East; ME = Middle East; Uncon = unconventional oil; Can = Canada; LAm = Latin America.

which largely assumed that oil production capacity could rise to meet demand regardless of current country plans. As a result, it called for unrealistically high oil demand and production capacity and very high levels of oil imports, and it created the impression of a potential global crisis in supply.

The importance of such modeling issues and assumptions for policymaking is clear from a brief comparison of the key conclusions in the 2004 and 2005 editions of the *IEO*. Actual total world production capacity in 2002 was 80.0 million barrels per day (mmbpd). The *IEO 2004* forecast that total world production capacity for 2025 would be 137.0 mmbpd for the low-price case, 126.1 mmbpd for the reference case, and 117.3 mmbpd for the high-price case.

In contrast, the *IEO 2005* forecasts total world production capacity in 2025 for the low-, medium-, and high-price cases as follows: 135.2 mmbpd for the low-price case, 122.2 mmbpd for the reference case, and 115.5 mmbpd for the high-price case. In both the 2004 and 2005 cases, the projected increase in total world production capacity is still significant. By 2010, it could increase from 14.6 mmbpd to as high as 21.6 mmbpd. The "high-price" case, however, is far easier to achieve in the real world than the "reference" or "low-price" cases.

As is clear from these numbers, as the price of oil decreases, production capacity increases. One notable exception is that the production capacities of countries that do not belong to the Organization of the Petroleum Exporting Countries (OPEC) have the opposite reaction to a change in the price of oil. OPEC countries largely drive this relationship between price and production capacity. From an economics point of view, a decline in the price of oil decreases the willingness of suppliers to produce and sell oil. The *IEO 2005*, however, shows the opposite effect for OPEC countries. One possible explanation is that OPEC countries control the price of oil with their quotas.

OPEC's actual production capacity in 2002 was 27.2 mmbpd. As table 7.1 shows, the *IEO 2004* forecast OPEC's production capacity in 2025 as 75.7 mmbpd for the low-price case, 61.5 mmbpd for the reference case, and 46.8 mmbpd for the high-price case. In contrast, the *IEO 2005* forecasts OPEC's production capacity in 2025 as follows:

72.80 mmbpd for the low-price case, 56.00 mmbpd for the reference case, and 40.40 mmbpd for the high-price case.

Price sensitivity in the current projection is indicated by the fact that the high-price level of production capacity for 2005 is 75.1 percent of the low-price estimate and 87.7 percent of the reference-case estimate. If the high-price level is compared with the 2004 case, the high-price level of production capacity for 2005 is only 53.4 percent of the low-price estimate and 65.7 percent of the reference-case estimate. This indicates that sustaining an average oil price of about $45 dollars per barrel would have an incredible impact in reducing past estimates of petroleum demand and supply.

SOLVING THE SUPPLY ISSUES RELATED TO MIDDLE EASTERN OIL

The potential impact of high oil prices in easing the strain on world oil supplies becomes clearer when one looks at the impact of oil prices on the need for Middle Eastern and North African conventional oil production capacity:

- The *IEO* analysis for 2004 called for major increases in Middle Eastern and North African oil production capacity.

- The *IEO 2005* forecasts that conventional Middle Eastern and North African production capacity in 2025 will be 51.1 mmbpd for the low-price case, 39.5 mmbpd for the reference case, and only 28.1 mmbpd for the high-price case.

These contrasts are even more striking for Saudi Arabia. For many years, most of OPEC's projected increase in production capacity in both the EIA and IEA models has been driven by Saudi Arabia. In recent times, the Saudi production capacity has received a lot of attention. As was noted earlier, some analysts have questioned the Kingdom's ability to meet sudden surges in demand because of its lack of spare production capacity, and others have estimated that Saudi production may be moving toward a period of sustained decline.

Saudi Arabia's oil production capacity in 2002 was 9.2 mmbpd. In 2004 its oil production capacity was roughly 9.0 to 10.5 mmbpd, and

Table 7.2
OPEC Oil Production Capacity, 2005–2025 (million barrels per day)

Country	2005 August	2010 Low	2010 Reference	2010 High	2025 Low	2025 Reference	2025 High
Al	1.380	2.200	2.000	1.800	3.700	2.800	2.200
Ind	0.945	1.200	1.500	1.400	1.500	1.500	1.400
Iran	4.000	4.800	4.000	4.000	6.600	5.000	4.500
Iraq	1.900	4.000	3.500	3.100	8.600	6.600	4.000
Ku	2.500	3.600	2.900	2.900	6.200	5.200	3.500
Li	1.635	2.200	2.000	1.800	3.900	2.900	2.200
Ni	2.450	3.300	2.600	2.400	6.400	3.900	2.900
Qa	0.800	0.800	0.600	0.600	0.900	0.800	0.800
Sau	10.50–11.00	15.600	14.000	10.400	20.400	16.300	11.000
UAE	2.400	4.000	3.300	3.400	7.000	5.400	4.000
Ven	2.500	4.600	3.500	3.200	7.300	5.600	3.900
Total	**31.005–31.505**	**46.300**	**39.900**	**35.000**	**72.500**	**56.000**	**40.400**

Source: Adapted by the authors from U.S. Energy Information Administration, *International Energy Outlook 2005.*

Note: Al = Algeria; Ind = Indonesia; Ku = Kuwait; Li = Libya; Ni = Nigeria; Qa = Qatar; Sau = Saudi Arabia; UAE = United Arab Emirates; Ven = Venezuela.

in 2005 it averaged 10.5 to 11 mmbpd. Like most of its predecessors, the *IEO* analysis for 2004 called for truly massive increases in Saudi oil. It forecast that Saudi Arabia's production capacity in 2025 would be 31.5 mmbpd for the low-price case, 22.5 mmbpd for the reference case, and 16.0 mmbpd for the high-price case.

As table 7.2 shows, the *IEO 2005* forecasts that Saudi Arabia's production capacity in 2025 will be 20.4 mmbpd for the low-price case, 16.3 mmbpd for the reference case, but only 11.0 mmbpd for the high-price case. Yet Saudi Arabia already plans to increase its production capacity to 12.5 mmbpd. Most analysts, including current and former Saudi Aramco officials, believe that 20.0 mmbpd is unattainable. One can argue that the Kingdom could reach this production capacity only if (1) major technological breakthroughs enhance the recovery of existing oil fields or help in finding new reservoirs, and (2) major supply disruptions force Saudi Arabia to meet the shortages in supply.

UNCERTAIN TRANSPARENCY AND UNCERTAIN CREDIBILITY

Table 7.1 shows similar, if less dramatic, trends for most of OPEC, and these trends apply to most of the non-OPEC states not shown in this table. Non-OPEC production capacity is also expected to show large increases in the midterm. These increases will come mainly from deepwater exploration in the North Sea, the Caspian Sea, the Gulf of Guinea, and the Gulf of Mexico. With advanced exploration and recovery technology, experts believe that offshore production can have significant influence on the world energy market in the middle to long terms.

High prices defer not only many of the issues related to future oil supply but also most of the issues related to any geopolitical competition for oil imports. The projected increases in production capacity at the high-price case for *IEO 2005* are far more achievable and sustainable in terms of the flow of global imports than any past EIA and IEA projections.

They would effectively eliminate most of rationale for the kind of struggle postulated in scenarios showing Chinese and Western competition for imports. The EIA does not explicitly address any of these issues in advancing its analysis of the high-price case, however, or provide the kind of data on overall energy balances and assumptions about supply and demand elasticities in other sectors of energy that would give such data meaning and credibility.

WORLD ECONOMIC GROWTH AND CONSUMPTION

The *IEO 2005* forecasts that total energy consumption will increase by 57 percent from 2002 to 2025. Much of this growth will be fueled by high economic growth in emerging markets in Asia. In fact, the *IEO 2005* claims that increases in energy consumption in the transitional economies and the mature market economies will be "modest." It forecasts that emerging economies will grow by 5.1 percent, mature economies will grow by 2.5 percent, and transitional economies will grow by 4.3 percent, as measured in the growth of gross domestic product in purchasing power terms.

World oil consumption in 2002 was 78.2 mmbpd, for the reference case; total world oil consumption is expected to rise to 103.2 mmbpd in 2010, to 111.0 mmbpd in 2020, and to 119.2 mmbpd in 2025. During the 2002–2025 period, China's consumption is forecast to rise from 5.2 mmbpd in 2002 to 9.2 mmbpd in 2010, 10.7 mmbpd in 2015, 12.3 mmbpd in 2020, and 14.2 mmbpd in 2025. Between 2002 and 2010, China's oil consumption will increase by 7.5 percent, but the growth rate will gradually decline.

The *IEO 2005* demand forecast adjusts for the higher prices (*IEO 2004* forecast that in 2025 total world oil consumption would be 121.0 mmbpd, compared with 119.2 mmbpd in the *IEO 2005* forecast). The projection, however, does not address the effect of conservation and alternative sources of energy. Moreover, the report does not give enough data for an analysis of demand–price elasticity.

One key example is renewables. The EIA forecasts in *IEO 2005* show that they will have little future impact on middle- to long-term world oil demand as measured in quadrillions of British thermal units (quads). If one excludes oil, natural gas, coal, and nuclear power, all other sources of energy only increase by an average of 1.9 percent in the reference case. As a result, their total contribution to world energy supply drops from 7.8 percent in 2002 to 7.6 percent in 2025—in spite of all the political focus on increasing such sources.

Because the *IEO 2005* does not examine the impact of high oil prices on world energy balances, there is no way to guess how much this would change if oil prices remained high, The two excursions the EIA does examine do not even hint at such effects. All other energy supplies drop to 7.3 percent of world supply in the "high-economic-growth" case, and to 7.5 percent in the "low-economic-growth" case.

Demand-Driven Models

Some argue that the energy market is demand driven, and that supply is largely exogenous. That is to say, overtime oil producers supply petroleum based on the level of demand in the global energy market.

This level of demand depends, among other things, on the level of economic growth, the price of oil, the existence of close substitutes or alternatives, and the preferences of consumers.

The models used by the EIA in its *IEO 2005*, for example, are demand driven. First, they forecast demand and then project the production capacity to meet this projected demand. The country's share of world's reserves is used to determine its share of the increase in production capacity, but demand-driven models do not take into account country-by-country plans. These models are based on the assumption that petroleum is produced to be consumed in terms of goods and services.

The first problem with this approach is that production capacity is entirely determined by assumptions about economic growth and the range of oil prices that the market will pay. If this range is unrealistic, then the whole model has a limited ability to predict. Demand-driven models do not lend themselves to parametric analysis of possible ranges of supply constraints. They have limited flexibility for sensitivity analysis, especially in terms of changing prices, technological changes in the industry, and potential changes in energy and foreign policy.

Demand-driven forecasts also tend to overestimate the influence of the price changes. Adjustments to demand and supply elasticities, however, are slow. In addition, these models do not seem to take into account "habit formation." If these models are demand driven, they must take into account persistence in changing habits that have formed over years. When the price of a barrel of oil jumped by 108 percent during the period 2001–2005, some analysts, for example, were surprised to see that demand did not adjust immediately.

Supply-Driven Models

Supply-driven models have the potential advantage of providing parametric and sensitivity analysis for demand, production, and production costs based on estimates of reserves and projected increases in production from technological improvements. They are also better built to take into account production and geopolitical risks and the impact of geostrategic risks on future flows of petroleum.

Supply-driven models can be of enormous importance to analysts and policymakers. The EIA, IEA, OPEC, and the U.S. Geological Survey (USGS) need to adapt such models to supplement their analysis and to combine their efforts with national energy agencies and companies in order to issue reports that are credible, transparent, and robust from a technical point of view.

This does not mean that demand-driven models do not have great value, but to fully understand the global petroleum market, energy experts must make a balancing effort to forecast supply and then determine what the demand will be.

This approach, as mentioned above, is more robust, but it requires access to credible data from suppliers or it needs to estimate many inputs, including production and transportation costs, the influence of new technological innovations on recovery and exploration rates, actual and possible reserves in the ground, and supply and demand elasticities.

Today, estimates of production capacity are largely based on "guesstimates" and "trusting" government claims. Estimating actual reserves in the abstract is difficult. Agencies such as the USGS, which look at reserves from a geological potential basis, have to update their estimates. Otherwise, the IEA and other organizations have to rely on the credibility and goodwill of the suppler countries to provide data, often without independent verification.

Current supply-driven models also suffer from the lack of price sensitivity analysis and the influence of technological improvements. Most energy models are not parametric or even semiparametric, and hence they limit the ability to test future changes in supply, demand, and prices. In addition, there is a lack of elasticity computations and estimates of the impact of efficiency, conservation, and alternatives.

It has been reported that the IEA is updating its estimates in its annual *World Energy Outlook* in November 2005. It is too soon to judge this report, but history has shown that the IEA reports lack credibility due to a lack of transparency, as is to be expected of any international body with many competing members, different reporting systems, and a lack of consensus on the importance of transparency.

MAJOR AREAS OF UNCERTAINTY IN THE ENERGY MODELING OF THE *IEO*

Reports such as the *IEO 2005* raise dramatic issues for energy policy planning, but they do not provide a meaningful basis for energy analysis in today's world. Adjusting the energy models to address all the implications of the high oil price is a vital and necessary first step. So is making all the assumptions and uncertainties involved in such an analysis transparent.

However, several other major areas also need improvement. It is all too clear that forecasts like the one provided by the *IEO* are difficult due to the complicated nature of the energy market, the limited hard country-by-country data, and the "immeasurable" risks involved in forecasting. There are areas where reports like the *IEO* could provide a better benchmark for the global energy market if they addressed the gaps and uncertainties left by the *IEO 2005*. The key gaps and areas of uncertainty in the *IEO 2005* include the following:

- The *IEO 2005* does not provide any parametric analysis of its oil price forecast.

- It does not provide sufficient explanation as to how the rates of economic growth interact with the price of oil and how the price elasticity of demand changes over time given an economic growth rate.

- It states that it has taken into account country-by-country plans in forecasting oil production capacity, but there is little explanation of how such plans have changed their forecast from the last one and how unrealistic those plans are.

- It does not make estimates of indirect imports of oil from the Gulf and other regions in terms of the energy required to produce finished goods. The United States, for example, indirectly imports very significant amounts of oil in the form of manufactures from Asian countries that are dependent on Middle Eastern oil imports.

- It does not provide a breakdown of the production forecasts of the countries of the former Soviet Union (FSU), on the Caspian

Sea, on the North Sea, in Africa, and in South and Central America. These areas, which are considered to have the greatest potential for enhancing production and new discoveries, should be broken down by country; for example, Russia should not be lumped in with smaller FSU states.

- It does not explicitly analyze technological improvements and their role in improving oil recovery and exploration for new oil reservoirs, developments that have significant effects on future oil supply and the oil market.

- It does not credibly explain the interactions among different oil prices, the level of oil supply and demand, and changes in the supply and demand of gas, coal, nuclear power, renewables, electricity, and conservation.

- It does not make an effort to determine the very different patterns of elasticity in supply and demand for gas, coal, nuclear power, renewables, electricity, and conservation that have to emerge over time if oil prices remain so much higher than in the past, or the major uncertainties that will inevitably result from such changes.

- It subjects the impact of growing Asian demand, especially by China, to only a limited sensitivity analysis. A Chinese recession or depression case is one such example.

- It treats major shifts in energy costs and different levels of economic growth largely as independent assumptions and variables.

- It does not address the impact of key options in U.S. energy policy or in the energy bill that was recently passed by Congress, especially options related to alternative energy sources and possible "strategies" to decrease dependence on foreign sources of energy.

- It does not analyze the effect of alternative source of energy or conservation, and it provides few data for any elasticity-based analysis.

- It does not analyze the impact of a persistently high oil price on the consumption of oil, production capacity, or conservation. Moreover, though it provides the three estimates (low, reference, and high), it provides no analysis of what they mean to the global energy market and how they are related to world energy demand.

- It includes limited historical or current data to enable us to make conclusions about the effect of conservation or alternative sources of energy on countries' production capacities.

One key aspect of these problems is the lack of any correlation between the EIA projections and the Bush administration's energy policies and the energy legislation passed by Congress. This is important in the case of the Bush administration, because the potential impact of its various energy policies has never been explicitly analyzed in the forecasts of either the *IEO* reports or the EIA's annual report on U.S. energy.

It is even more important in the case of the recent energy bill passed by Congress, because if the *IEO 2005* projection is correct, a sustained increase in oil prices would have far more of an impact on U.S. energy needs than the measures in the bill, which could easily waste some $40 billion to $60 billion in needless pork and pointless subsidies to special interests that would be far better left to market forces. A less incompetent and corrupt approach to energy policy—based on public modeling and analysis of the metrics of each action by the federal government—would have far more of an impact on U.S. energy imports, although any realistic projection of the impact of the Bush administration's policies, the energy bill, and/or high oil prices would still not change the level of U.S. strategic dependence on oil imports.

In any case, the United States' search for "energy independence" borders on the analytically absurd. America will be critically dependent on direct and indirect oil imports through 2025. In the case of the Bush administration's policies and energy bill, not only will the potential impact be limited, but the basic policy is fatally flawed. It assumes that America's problems can be solved by focusing on American imports. The reality is that the United States is becoming steadily more dependent on the global economy and on the global flow of energy imports. Playing with marginal reductions in U.S. oil imports is of virtually no strategic importance at all.

STILL THE BEST GAME IN TOWN

It should be stressed that so far, the Energy Information Administration is the only major agency to even begin to address the prospect of sustained high oil prices and to respond to real-world trends. Furthermore, the structural problems in the EIA's projections are no different from the demand-driven modeling of the IEA and OPEC—and that used in virtually all government reports. In fact, the EIA's modeling and analysis are far more transparent than that of the IEA—which generally sets very low standards in this area.

The future of energy is of enormous importance, and reports can provide significant insight into the energy market. The *IEO 2005* has attempted to fill the gaps that existed in the *IEO 2004*. Unfortunately, it highlights the critical impact that oil prices may have on world oil demand and supply and then does not analyze these effects on any other aspect of energy supply and demand or on energy balances.

Moreover, the *IEO* does not cover many important areas, such as the role of technological improvement and the effect of alternative sources of energy on production capacity and world energy demand, respectively. As such, the EIA's failure is even more critical because the IEA and OPEC have so far done nothing meaningful to update their analyses to deal with the possibility of long-term "high-price" cases.

Notes

[1] U.S. Energy Information Administration (EIA), *International Energy Outlook 2005*, July 2005.

ABOUT THE AUTHORS

Anthony H. Cordesman holds the Arleigh A. Burke Chair in Strategy at CSIS. He is also a national security analyst for ABC News and a frequent commentator on National Public Radio and the BBC. His television commentary has been prominently featured during the Iraq War, the conflict in Kosovo, the fighting in Afghanistan, and the Gulf War.

Prior to CSIS, Cordesman served in numerous government positions, including as national security assistant to Senator John McCain of the Senate Armed Services Committee, as director of intelligence assessment in the Office of the Secretary of Defense, as civilian assistant to the deputy secretary of defense, and as director of policy and planning for resource applications at the Department of Energy. He has also served in the State Department and on NATO International Staff and has had many foreign assignments, including posts in Lebanon, Egypt, and Iran, with extensive work in Saudi Arabia and the Gulf.

Cordesman is the author of more than 20 books on U.S. security policy, energy policy, and the Middle East, as well as a four-volume series on the lessons of modern war. His most recent books include *The Challenge of Biological Terrorism* (CSIS, 2005); *Iraqi Security Forces: A Strategy for Success* (Praeger/CSIS, 2005); *The Israeli-Palestinian War: Escalating to Nowhere* (Praeger/CSIS, 2005); *National Security in Saudi Arabia: Threats, Responses, and Challenges*, with Nawaf Obaid (Praeger/CSIS, 2005); *Iran's Developing Military Capabilities* (CSIS, 2005); *The War after the War: Strategic Lessons of Iraq and Afghanistan* (CSIS,

2004); *The Military Balance in the Middle East* (Praeger/CSIS, 2004); *Energy Developments in the Middle East* (Praeger/CSIS, 2004); *The Iraq War: Strategy, Tactics, and Military Lessons* (Praeger/CSIS, 2003); *Saudi Arabia Enters the 21st Century* (Praeger/CSIS, 2003); *The Lessons of Afghanistan: War Fighting, Intelligence, and Force Transformation* (CSIS, 2002); and *Terrorism, Asymmetric Warfare, and Weapons of Mass Destruction* (Praeger/CSIS, 2002).

Khalid R. Al-Rodhan is a fellow with the Burke Chair and coauthor with Cordesman of several books on energy security and military strategy, including *Gulf Military Forces in an Era of Asymmetric War* (Praeger/CSIS, forthcoming).